LAUGH
with
HUGH TROY

World's Greatest Practical Joker

LAUGH
with
Hugh Troy

World's greatest practical joker

A happy memoir by
Con Troy

Including an
Epigraph and Illustrations by
Tom Wolfe

Additional Illustrations by
Paul Gurney and David Seavey
and
Photographs by
Barrett Gallagher

TROJAN BOOKS

TROJAN BOOKS

1330 Cleveland Ave.
Wyomissing, Pa. 19610

Dedicated

to those friends of Hugh Troy,
over a hundred,
who showed their affection for him
through their memoirs.
They grew into this book.

An Epigraph
to
My friend, Hugh Troy

Hugh Troy was the King of Hoaxers, a gigantic personality, our all-time, free-style, practical joke champion, the envy and ideal of practical joke-smiths the world over. He was an artist of the practical joke, with a refined touch and a sense of the profoundly satirical. All of this was in addition to the main business of his life: painting murals, writing and illustrating books, serving his country in mysterious ways, and delighting his friends with his warmth and humor.

Tom Wolfe

Hugh Troy

List of Illustrations

Hugh Troy—as pictured by Tom Wolfe — Title page

Hugh Troy — Frontispiece

The Cornell Arts Quad — 14

The Library Tower — 15

Professor "Pa" Martin — 17

The drafting room in White Hall — 18

Professor Ranum — 20

Beebe Lake — 23

White Hall — 33

Freshman architects posing for their "class picture" — 34

The "Dunking Tank" — 36

Ezra Cornell and his footprints — 37

"Andy" White and his footprints — 37

The "Saloon de Garboon," as pictured by Paul Gurney — 40

"My poor baby brother . . ." by Paul Gurney — 42

A feature article in the *Globe and Square Dealer* — 50

The *Syracuse American* page-wide spread — 51

The editorial board "before and after" — 52

Hugh's New Year's card — 54

One of Hugh's murals in the former Heigh-Ho Club, New York — 57

The lower concourse, Grand Central Station, New York — 58

The apartment house at 8 West Seventy-sixth Street — 61

The apartment house at 16 Minetta Lane — 69

Decorating the globe of the world, Daily News Building, New York — 70

"Troy's Thirty Acres" — 73

The apartment house at 151 East Forty-ninth Street — 74

Hugh's "Sidewalk Superintendent" card — 76

". . . he might flop into his chair and light a cigarette." — 78

Hugh's 1931 Christmas card — 84

The "Fountain of Youth" mural in Radio City Music Hall, New York — 85

A portion of Hugh's mural in the former Savoy Plaza Hotel, New York — 87

"Van Gogh's Ear," as pictured by Tom Wolfe 89
One of Hugh's murals in the former Mark Twain Hotel, Elmira, N.Y. 92
The telegram Hugh's Aunt Rose sent to Professor Troy 93
A Hugh Troy mural design for a hotel in the Catskills 96
Hugh's mural in the former Toffenetti restaurant, Times Square 103
An illustration from *Maud for a Day* 106
Hugh pauses while working on the Metropolitan Life mural 107
"Ducks in the Organ," as pictured by David Seavey 111
An illustration from *The Chippendale Dam* 112
Lieutenant Troy 119
"The Flypaper Reports," as pictured by Tom Wolfe 122
An illustration from *Five Golden Wrens* 125
General Curtis LeMay 126
". . . a lizard guards our tent at night" 134
". . . feathered, bespectacled creatures that are very kind." 134
The Cuevas mansion 137
Hugh's home in Garrison, N.Y. 139
Hugh and his Ivy Room mural, Willard Straight Hall, Cornell. 140
A painting by "the Number One Ghost" 152
The British author and lecturer, Stephen Potter 155
Dave Garroway, a former host of the Today Show 164
Swapping tales of Hugh Troy 175

LAUGH
with
HUGH TROY

World's Greatest Practical Joker

One

In September of 1925 — right in the middle of the "Roaring Twenties" — Americans were "keeping cool with Coolidge," laughing at Charlie Chaplin in *The Gold Rush,* and dancing the Charleston. And in Ithaca, N.Y. thousands of wide-eyed high school graduates humming "Don't Bring Lulu" or "Collegiate" were descending on the city to enter Cornell University. The Cornell campus buzzed with activity as eager freshmen explored its dozens of buildings.

As thousands had before him, one new student had just registered in Morrill Hall.

"Very good, sir," said the clerk. "Your fee's paid and everything seems in order. Now, for architecture, you'll attend classes in White Hall, just two buildings away. Please sign here and take this envelope over there. Room 101."

"Yes, sir. Thank you very much."

Leaving Morrill Hall behind, the fledgling architect drank in the scene that would greet his eyes for the next five years. Far below, beyond the distant rooftops of the city — Cornell was built on Ithaca's East Hill — stretched the endless silvery sheen of Lake Cayuga. Ahead, on his left, came McGraw Hall, then a statue of the founder of the university, Ezra Cornell, then White Hall. A four-story structure of native stone, its severe lines graced only by a mantle of meandering ivy, White Hall, like its neighbors, embodied the stern Quaker character of Cornell.

Students by one, twos, and threes bustled along many paths

". . . a spacious quadrangle, the Arts Quad."

crisscrossing a spacious quadrangle on the new freshman's right: the Arts Quad. Shining through the branches of tall, graceful elms, the sun dappled the broad, green carpet of the Quad. Fall was in the air; its first tawny leaves tumbled lightly in the breeze, a breeze bringing a melody from the library tower chimes.

"Quite a place," thought the newcomer. "I'm going to like it here, I'm a lucky guy."

But suddenly he was plunged into sadness. On the ground in front of White Hall sat an amputee, legs obviously cut off at the hips, poor fellow. His grey topcoat was spread around him on the ground. He wore dark glasses and held a tin cup.

At the sight, the new arrival dropped all thoughts of his good fortune. His mind framed the question, "How can God be so unjust?"

The luckless chap on the ground evidently heard his footsteps. He thrust his cup forward. "Any spare change, mister?" he pleaded.

"Anything will help."

The freshman fished in his pocket. He found only a dime. It would have to do. He dropped it in the cup.

"Thank you. Thank you kindly, sir."

Standing in the doorway of White Hall, an elderly man pushed a broom. He stepped back to let the new student in.

"Room 101, please?"

"Second door on your right."

"Thank you."

"I see you lost some money."

"I . . . lost money?" said the freshman, puzzled.

"Yeah." The old man smiled. "That fellow out there."

". . . a melody from the Library Tower chimes."

"Oh, I felt sorry for him," the newcomer explained. "Life sure gave him a raw deal."

"Not exactly." The broom-wielder chuckled. "That's Hugh Troy. He's a junior — no, a senior this year. You're the fifth freshman he's hoodwinked."

"Troy? But his legs —? I don't see —"

"Legs?" He's standing in a manhole."

And thus, the new student — as had so many before him — met and was vanquished by Hugh Troy, destined to become the King of Hoaxers.

Three years before that episode, Hugh Troy had also enrolled in Cornell's college of architecture. Students there soon came to recognize his lithe, lanky figure. Easily the tallest fellow in the college, he ambled through the halls with a distinctive, loose, gangling gait, his head often cocked to one side. His short, curly black hair surmounted a bland baby face apparently completely innocent of guile.

Some tall people are self-conscious about their height and may even slouch a bit in an attempt to appear less conspicuous. Not Hugh. He liked to keep the record straight and legitimately claimed to be the tallest man on campus. And every year since he entered, new students aspiring to the heights in architecture confronted Hugh's challenge — a mark high on a wall in White Hall with this note below:

HUGH TROY '27 Arch.

6 ft. 6 in.

No one ever reached his mark as long as it remained legible.

In White Hall, as young Troy and his classmates soon found out, Professor "Pa" Martin was king. For, besides teaching architecture and drawing, he was the building overseer. Martin's penetrating eyes behind small, rimless glasses, his grey hair, mustache, and Van

"In White Hall . . . Professor 'Pa' Martin was king."

Dyke beard gave him a forbidding appearance that belied his innate kindliness. That kindliness was sorely tried by the antics of his students, who often had Troy as their ringleader.

Dividing his time between his lecture room on the second floor and the drafting room directly above on the third floor, Pa often found himself with more than he could handle and Hugh couldn't resist such opportunities.

White Hall being an old structure, a crack had opened up in the ceiling of Pa's lecture room. Before each lecture, which he gave every other morning, he would go through the same ritual. Walking in, he'd stand there, arms akimbo, staring at the crack in the ceiling for a minute. Then, in an ominous tone of voice, he'd announce his verdict: "It's getting bigger! Fellows, don't walk under that. Old building, you know. Can't tell what might happen."

Sometimes while Pa would be lecturing a class, Hugh and his fellow-students in the drafting room above would be stamping around too much or having a little roughhouse. Pa's ceiling would shake and bits of plaster would fall down on him while he was talking.

He'd stop lecturing and come running up the stairs. "Boys, boys," he'd exclaim. "How many times do I have to tell you? This is an old building. The ceiling below can take only so much. And I'll tell you this. If anything happens because of your horseplay, I guarantee you'll pay for it. And you can bet your life on that." Then back down he'd go.

Hearing him complain like that gave Hugh an idea. He made a still life on a large piece of white canvas, a replica of part of a fallen ceiling. Around a jet-black "hole" in the center he glued pieces of lath with jagged edges sticking out at odd angles and little slabs of broken plaster hanging down. One night, with some friends helping

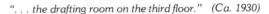

". . . the drafting room on the third floor." (Ca. 1930)

Hugh with a ladder, he pasted the still life on the ceiling right over Pa's lectern. Before leaving, they threw rubble, chunks of plaster, and pieces of broken lath all over Pa's podium and over the floor.

The next morning the perpetrators were in the drafting room when Pa entered his lecture room. He saw the mess on the floor, looked at the ceiling, then came bounding up the stairs. *"At last you've done it!"* he bellowed. *"*A big chunk of ceiling has crashed to the floor and I'm lucky I wasn't under it when it fell."

Taking out a notebook, he started writing. "I'm taking your names. You'll all pay for this," he said, "and don't you forget it. I'm going to call Charley Curtis, our superintendent of buildings and grounds, right now. He'll have the ceiling fixed and bill each of you for your share of the cost." Then he stamped into his office and slammed the door.

A little later, Hugh posted two classmates outside Pa's office with drawings under their arms. Their job, in case Pa opened his door, was to keep him in his office, ostensibly to settle some disagreement they had cooked up. While they guarded Pa, Hugh and the rest of his crew got out the ladder, took down the fake, and cleaned up the room.

In about an hour, Charley Curtis approached the building. He came in, found Pa standing in the hall outside his office, and asked, "What's your trouble?"

Pa glared at him. "Trouble? I'll show you trouble. You just come with me." He marched Curtis over to his lecture room, gave the door a push, and said, "Just take a look in there."

Curtis walked in, gazed at a room in perfect condition, and said, "What's wrong?" Pa walked up, then just stood there with his mouth open, staring at the ceiling. He couldn't even speak.

Hugh Troy had scored again.

Hugh's brand of playfulness was far removed from the tack on the chair, the "snake" in the peanut brittle tin, the bucket of water over the door. No, nothing so crude. Loving, gentle, kind, his pranks

". . . Arthur Ranum, the legendary absent-minded professor."

were benign, subtle, sophisticated. Gifted with an ebullient personality and a sharp eye for the ridiculous, he had a rare, inborn appreciation of the humorous potential of a scene.

Professors, of course, are always fair game for students. But Hugh's were so serious that few pupils had the temerity to trick them. Young Troy's stunts, though, were so ingenious and delightful that none of the professors ever got mad. Instead, they wound up laughing right along with him. They enjoyed not only that side of Hugh but also his gentleness and his friendliness.

Arthur Ranum, a short, handsome good-humored man who taught Hugh's solid geometry class, typified the legendary absentminded professor. Ranum often buried his acquiline nose in a book while walking on the campus, and if he suspected it might rain, always put on his raincoat and rubbers in the morning.

One misty morning, true to form, the prof showed up in his wet-weather togs and left them in the hall where everyone left their outdoor gear. Apparently Hugh had been waiting for just such a day. He made an excuse to leave the room and, while the professor's back was turned, beckoned to his classmate, Stilwell Brown, to follow him.

A few minutes after Hugh left, Brownie also left. Around a bend in the hall he found Hugh sitting on a stool holding a can of paint and a pair of rubbers. "Hugh, what are you do —? *Whose rubbers are those?*"

"Shhh. Pipe down. They're Ranum's. Just having a little fun with the old fellow."

"What's the paint for?"

"You'll see in a minute. Stand over there at the corner of the hall and keep your eyes open, will you, while I work on these?" "While I stood guard," Brownie related later, "Hugh decorated the rubbers with white paint so each one looked like a bare human foot. While painting away, he kept chuckling and slapping his thigh as he always did when he was enjoying himself. A little later, when the paint had dried, he covered the rubbers with powdered lampblack and put them back in place."

That noon, during a drizzle, Ranum started walking home. The lampblack washed away. Everyone he met seemed unusually friendly, smiling at him, grinning, even giggling. Finally a coed worked up enough nerve to talk to him.

"Professor Ranum?"

"Yes?"

"Should you be walking around in the rain in your bare feet?"

A perfect Hugh Troy achievement.

The young Trojan also had his serious side, a deep interest in art. Instead of playing basketball or baseball, Hugh was always drawing or painting. He especially admired and tried to emulate his friend, Louis Agassiz Fuertes, one of America's greatest bird painters.

A great naturalist and veteran of many a safari, Fuertes had decorated his studio with exotic flora and fauna including stuffed birds, tribal masks, a blowgun, and the foot of a rhinoceros that had been hollowed out to serve as a wastebasket.

Intrigued by the unusual object, Hugh dreamed up a new use for it. Borrowing it from Fuertes one winter, he weighted it down with scrap iron and tied it in the middle of a rope about thirty feet long. Then he waited for proper weather conditions.

One night, after a couple of inches of snow had fallen, Troy and a friend started across the Cornell campus, each holding one end of the rope. As they walked along, they raised and lowered the waste-basket at the proper intervals while moving it from side to side so as to make a trail of huge footprints in the snow.

Students on their way to classes next morning found the strange impressions and told one of their instructors about them. He puzzled over the prints.

"Well," he said, "a cow or horse didn't make *those* tracks. The footprints are too big. We'd better ask the professor of zoology to come down here."

"Hmmm," said the professor. "Those tracks were made by a . . . let me see . . . ." He peered into his handbook. "Some foreign animal," he announced.

"Foreign animal?" asked a local newspaper reporter who had joined the investigation. "What kind of animal?"

"Well, it doesn't seem possible but it must be a rhinoceros."

"*Rhinoceros?* You sure?"

"Yep. No other animal makes a footprint like that. Here it is, right in the book."

"Well, what became of it? Hey, let's follow its tracks and find it."

The rhino hunters took off on the trail. Leaving the campus, the tracks led to Beebe Lake, Cornell's water reservoir.

"There they go," exclaimed the professor, waving his arm, "over the ice to that hole."

"Must have fallen in," said the reporter.

"Looks that way. So heavy it crashed through the ice."

Scuttling back to his desk, the reporter punched out a story under a headline that shook up the city of Ithaca:

RHINOCEROS DROWNS IN BEEBE LAKE

Half the people served by Beebe Lake stopped drinking tap water. Those that did drink it didn't care for it. "Tastes too much like rhinoceros," they complained.

They felt better a few weeks later though. Hugh couldn't keep the

"... *the tracks led to Beebe Lake and over the ice to a hole.*"

secret any longer and told his friends what had really happened. As usual, he was forgiven.

Hugh often visited Ezra Cornell's old home on the campus which had rooms that were rented to architectural students. The "Architects' House," as it was called, was popular with Troy and his coterie for a very good reason. It was a regular Friday night stop for the local bootlegger, that unique offspring of Volstead's "Great Experiment," Prohibition. His bottled-in-barn tongue-loosener — usually straight alcohol diluted with water and colored with caramel — was real high-octane. The young architects learned that the hard way at their regular Saturday night happy hours.

For one of those binges, "Uncle" Prof Seymour, who taught architecture, came over to lift a few with the boys. With handsome, regular features, a full head of black hair parted on one side, a steady gaze, and a small, closely-trimmed mustache, the professor could easily be mistaken for a stage celebrity.

Succumbing slowly to the effect of the bootlegger's beverage, Seymour became garrulous. He started telling the group about the new house he had just built in the suburb of Cayuga Heights, and he promised he would soon have all of them over to see it.

Finally, realizing his potion had more punch than he had anticipated, Uncle mumbled a fuzzy farewell, pulled himself to his feet, and tottered off for home.

Hugh then persuaded his pals they should inspect Uncle's new home that very weekend. Walking to Cayuga Heights the next morning, they knocked on the prof's door. Uncle, in his bathrobe, greeted them with, "Well, what do *you* kids want?"

"Why, Professor Seymour," said Hugh, "don't you remember last night you invited us all over to your new house for breakfast?"

"I *did?*"

"Sure, just before you left for home."

"Oh! — Well! — Why . . . why . . . come on in."

Seymour called to his wife and the two started bustling around the kitchen, cracking eggs and mixing pancake batter. While this was going on, Hugh wandered to the far end of their living room where some new furniture his wife had ordered had been delivered the day before. The price tags had not been removed. The opportunity was too good for Hugh to miss.

With one eye on the kitchen, Hugh altered the price tags. On a chair, he changed the tag reading $110 to $190. On a sofa, he changed the tag from $350 to $450 and so on.

After breakfast, the students adjourned to the living room. What with his attending the party and coming home late, Uncle hadn't had much chance to look at his new furniture. So, while everyone else chatted, he examined it. Suddenly he turned around, made for the kitchen, and started arguing with Mrs. Seymour. Hugh began to grin. As the voices from the kitchen became louder, Hugh's grin became broader.

"Let's beat it," he said. Hugh and his pals left for home, leaving the Seymours to fight it out until the professor would finally realize the trick that had been played on him.

Two

Hugh would often invite his companions to his home at 305 Oak Avenue, a spacious, three-story structure built by his father, who was Cornell's professor of dairy chemistry. Most of Hugh's fellow-architects remember his home as the scene of his frequent Charette meetings. Charette was their coined term for an intense, joint effort to meet a project deadline. In a typical session, Hugh and his friends would start by tackling the job at hand. With some progress made, the group would take time out to exchange stories, spin yarns, or discuss campus issues or personalities.

Such a recess was always the most enjoyable part of the evening as Hugh was not only a delightful entertainer but also a charming conversationalist. While laughing generously at other people's flights of wit, he would often drop a remark in his low-voiced inimitable style. After their break, everyone would usually get right back to work. As many remember, though, one of Hugh's meetings didn't turn out that way.

Before that affair, Hugh told his mother, Mary Troy, a sweet, kindly, Irish soul, that eight or ten of his friends would be coming to the house. "It will be a long evening of hard work, Mother," he explained. "Would you mind setting something out for a late-night snack?"

That afternoon, Mrs. Troy had Nellie, their maid, buy a package of bacon and two dozen eggs. Nellie and Hugh's young cousin, Edith Cuervo (as an orphan, she lived with the Troys), then set out a supply of food on the kitchen counter. After Hugh's friends had gathered, the family went to bed.

During the night, the house echoed with so much raucous laughter and noise from the Charette party that Edith was awake for hours, sleeping only in fits and starts. About six in the morning, she finally was sleeping soundly. But she was suddenly awakened by a sharp knock on her door.

"Who is it?" she asked.

"It's me, Nellie. Can you get up, Edith?" Nellie sounded upset.

"What is it, Nellie?"

"Come downstairs. I want you to see — "

Throwing on her housecoat, Edith ran after the maid, who was already halfway down to the kitchen where Hugh had held his party.

"Oh, my God!" said Edith, coming through the door. One whole wall, the floor, and part of the ceiling was plastered with egg yolks, egg whites, and eggshells.

"Oh, Edith," moaned Nellie, "I would *never* want Mrs. Troy to see this."

"Oh, Lord, no. But she's still asleep, thank heavens. Let's see if we can't clean it up before she comes down." They started picking up eggshells.

"I'll get a stepladder," said Nellie.

Nellie climbed the ladder and started washing the walls. While cleaning the furniture and scrubbing the floor, Edith wondered what had happened at Hugh's party.

Later her curiosity was satisfied. She found out that the group had nearly completed their work when Hugh's eyelids had begun drooping — he had slaved on the project for twenty hours straight — and he had started nodding. His student guests prevailed on him to take a nap which stretched into an all-night snooze.

Waiting for his return, his friends, after lapping up some needled beer someone had brought, were feeling too happy for work and turned to horseplay. While they were polishing off most of the bacon and eggs, one of them had spied the ventilating fan spinning over the kitchen sink. "What would happen if an egg hit that fan?" he asked.

"Why, it would be blown back into the room," someone answered.

"Oh, no," said another, "it would be thrown to the side of the fan."

To settle the argument, they agreed on a test. Those who thought the egg would be thrown to the side stood in front of the fan. The others, who thought the egg would be blown back into the room, stood at the side.

The boys in front of the fan then hurled their eggs. The first half-dozen missed the target entirely, exploding on the kitchen wall. The next one was a clean hit, the fan throwing a yellow streak around the floor, walls, and ceiling, and all over the boys standing at the side. Of course, they lost the argument.

By nine o'clock, after much scraping and scrubbing, Edith and Nellie had the place fairly well cleaned. After putting away the scouring powder, cleaning cloths, and ladder, they were nearly ready to collapse with fatigue when they heard footsteps.

In walked Mrs. Troy. "Good morning, Edith," she said. "Oh," — she stifled a small yawn — "excuse me. Why — ah — did Hugh and his boys get their work all done?"

"Yes, Mother," replied Edith. "They got along fine. Nellie and I are just straightening things up a bit."

"Oh, that makes me happy. And I see the eggs are all gone. I'm so glad they enjoyed them."

Besides Edith, Professor Troy's home was a haven for Hugh's Grandmother Troy who had long outlived her husband, John. Having a poor memory, besides being afflicted with a hearing loss, she became, especially during Hugh's high school days, a victim of his playful but harmless deceptions. One of these was "getting grandmother behind."

During summer vacation, Hugh's father and mother would leave for a few week's trip, part business, part pleasure. They'd leave the children — Elinor, Hugh's young brother, Francis, Edith, and Hugh — with Grandma. As soon as his father and mother left, Hugh would begin on Grandma by mixing up her calendar. She was fond of reading the New York Times in the morning. Usually she would fall asleep by the third or fourth page. Hugh would then replace the paper with the one from the day before. If she fell asleep on Friday, when she woke up it would be Thursday. After doing this a few times, Hugh actually got Grandma to the point where Wednesday became Sunday to her.

"Elinor! — Hugh!" she called to them on Wednesday morning. "Don't you know it's getting late? It's almost time for church."

"Yes, Grandma," they replied.

Then Grandma visited Nellie in the kitchen who was in on the scheme. "Nellie, are you getting the chicken ready for dinner?"

"Yes, Mrs. Troy," Nellie said. "It'll be ready when they come back from church."

The children dressed and left for a long walk and, after they came back, Hugh got out the Sunday papers which they had hidden for four days. Then they all sat down to dinner and Grandma led them in prayer.

It was harder to bring Grandma back up to date when the time approached for the return of Father and Mother. They had to shuffle the papers in reverse fashion. Still, they managed to do it. Grandma was back on the same schedule as the rest of the world when the parents returned.

As the years rolled by, poor Grandma's hearing became worse. And, because she had now become very near-sighted, she didn't take much pleasure in reading. But she did enjoy visits from Agnes

McGraham, a sweet, modest young girl who lived nearby.

She lost even that pleasure, however, for Agnes left to enter a convent. Grandma missed her greatly and longed to see her again. Hugh found a way to satisfy her wish and got Edith to help him carry it out. Let us add that, since Agnes had left, the Troys had taken in some students, young men going to Cornell, as roomers upstairs.

After making sure Grandma was sitting in the living room, Hugh dressed up like a girl, went outside, and rang the bell. Edith went to the door, let him in, then said, "Grandma, someone's here to see you." She left the room but listened outside the door, wondering what Hugh would say.

Hugh walked slowly into the room. "Hello, Mrs. Troy," he said in falsetto.

"Who . . . who . . . who is it?"

"Why, it's *me*. Agnes McGraham."

"Why, Agnes! It's so good to see you! But you . . . you . . . you've changed. And I . . . I thought you were in the convent?"

"Yes, I was. But I just couldn't *stand* it. That darned place was *too slow* for me. Oh, yes, I understand you have . . . ah . . . *students* upstairs."

"Why, yes, Agnes, we do."

"Well, couldn't you . . . ah . . . call some of them down?"

"Why, Agnes! That's not *like* you."

"Yes, I know. But that darned convent *changed* me."

Pretty soon, Hugh said he'd have to go. After hearing Grandma say, "Goodbye, Agnes," Edith stepped into the room.

Grandma whirled around to her. "Edith!" she snapped. "Why, that Agnes McGraham has gotten so bold. Imagine her coming in here and asking to see the students upstairs. The *students!* I can't believe it of her. She's gotten so awfully *bold!*"

Hugh Troy inspired his Cornell classmates to take a more relaxed view of life and use a little more fun to spice their daily existence. His philosophy was that humor can drive away more troubles and heal more dissension among people than anything else. And humor was needed in his day as much as it is needed now.

When ill feeling was rife and the college was uptight, a Hugh Troy stunt would often wash it all away in gales of laughter, leaving everyone relaxed and ready to face life anew. Testifying to his originality, some of his feats were enjoyed so much that students still repeat them from year to year.

One of these is an annual architects' event, photographing the freshman class. Such an affair was easy for Hugh to arrange as his uncle, John P. Troy, was the Cornell photographer. With his studio near the Arts Quad, his services were much in demand for the many photos required by campus groups. Tall, gaunt, with sparse gray hair, rimless glasses, and a quiet, businesslike manner, he was a lifelong bachelor with pursed lips and old-maidish mannerisms.

Invoking his uncle's name, Hugh staged a picture taking ceremony that deviated from the conventional script. A week beforehand, he posted bulletins on every floor of White Hall announcing:

ATTENTION FRESHMAN ARCHITECTS!
ANNUAL CLASS PICTURE BY TROY STUDIO
Please report to Room 100 at 4:00 P.M.
Monday to register. Suit, shirt,
tie required.

The seniors and juniors had formerly been treating the frosh like scum. But now they greeted them as they passed in the halls.

"Hey, Frosh!" Hugh's shill, George Siebenthaler, would say when he spotted a freshman going by. "Did you see that notice about your class picture?"

"Right, Mr. Siebenthaler. I'll be there."

"Good. See you there. Like to meet your friends. Good chance to get acquainted."

"Oh, we'd like that."

Came time for the freshmen to assemble. "Listen, fellows," said George. "Anything you want to know, don't be afraid to ask. Now, on the register, be sure to print your name in capital letters. And *don't forget,* put down how many prints you want."

Herding the innocents in their freshly pressed suits and new ties out to the front steps, the seniors spread them out so everyone would show up well. The photographer was already in position.

"*. . . he posted bulletins on every floor of White Hall.*"

Hunched over in back of his camera and tripod, he had a black cloth over his head.

Glancing up to the third floor windows, the freshmen could make out the beaming faces of their newfound pals, the seniors and juniors.

Up went the photographer's arm. From under the black cloth

came a yell: "All right, fellows! *Big smile!*"

A happier bunch you'd never see — for a few seconds.

SPLASH! SPLUSH! SPLASH! Falling from buckets in the hands of the upperclassmen three floors above, a torrent of water drenched the dismayed victims.

Out in front, the photographer threw off his black cloth, folded his tripod with a smile, and strolled away. It was Hugh. He had borrowed the camera from his Uncle John.

". . . a torrent of water drenched the dismayed victims."
Hugh's hoax is still staged at Rand Hall, Cornell.

Most of the new boys took Hugh's "class picture" good-naturedly. But once in a while a "mama's boy" or an overly sensitive freshman might object. If he made himself obnoxious by carrying his case to the faculty, he became a marked man.

For such behavior — or other serious crimes — he would become a candidate for "the Dunking Tank." The tank, twelve feet long by ten feet wide, was located on the third floor of White Hall. Usually filled with three feet of water, it was used for plotting landscape contours.

Convening a kangaroo court with his friends sitting in judgment, Hugh would present his charges:

"Fred Short, you're charged with complaining to the professors about how we've been treating you. Is that any way to repay us for all our kindness?"

"May I say —"

"Don't interrupt! Gentlemen of the jury! You are all aware of the generous way we've always treated Mr. Short and the despicable way he has repaid us. What's your verdict, guilty or not guilty?"

"*Guilty!*"

"Okay. Let's get this over with. George, pull that drawing table over here near the tank." Propping drawing boards up on stepladders, the jurors slanted them toward the tank. (In the winter, its contents might include three or four inches of snow and slush the boys had scraped off the roof.)

"All right, Short," said Hugh. "Up you go."

"But Mr. Troy —"

"*Up!*"

Up he went and *Splash!* into the drink, clothes and all.

Hugh's methods for keeping the frosh in line never brought any objections from the professors. In fact, they tacitly approved, feeling no doubt, that the upperclassmen could handle discipline as well as the faculty.

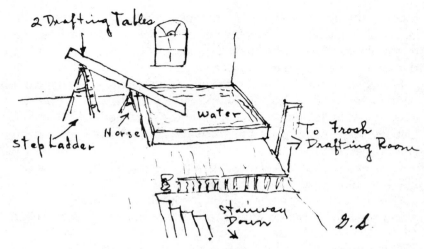

"Propping drawing boards up on stepladders, the jurors slanted them toward the tank."

Another exploit links Hugh's name in a sentimental way with Ezra Cornell and "Andy" White, the first president of the university. Their statues, facing each other on opposite sides of the Arts Quad, are connected by a sidewalk.

As Hugh and his architect companion, Don Hershey, were strolling past Cornell's statue one afternoon, Hugh paused. He had an idea. He outlined his scheme to Hershey who readily agreed.

They met again at midnight. Don carried an old dishpan and Hugh, wearing a pair of galoshes, began busily stirring a gallon can of white paint.

"Let's start near old man Cornell," said Hugh. "Lay your dishpan down here."

Hugh then poured paint into the pan until it was half an inch deep. Dipping his right foot into the paint, he removed it, pressed it on the sidewalk, then did the same with his left foot. Repeating the process, with Don moving the pan along and replenishing the paint,

Hugh soon had a trail of footprints showing Cornell leaving his statue and walking toward the center of the Quad.

"He gave White a similar trail of footprints," recalls Don, "then painted a large square, or 'rendezvous' in the center of the sidewalk. Hugh had the easy end of it. But for me, it was back-breaking work."

The ghostly footprints can still be seen today, for students repaint them from year to year in memory of another of Hugh Troy's famous stunts.

". . . a trail of footprints showing Cornell leaving his statue . . ." "He gave White a similar trail of footprints, then painted a large square or 'rendezvous' in the center of the sidewalk."

Little feuds were always springing up between the engineers and the architects, who had a reputation for doing kooky things, such as their annual Snake Dance, something like a Chinese Snake Parade.

That was only one of the reasons the engineers figured the architects for a bunch of genuine screwballs, everyone crazy as a cockroach. And they didn't mind telling that to anyone who would listen. Hugh heard about it and got his fellow-architects together one day.

"I'm fed up with those stupid engineers," he told them, "calling us crazy all the time. We'll show 'em who's crazy." He said he'd found an old whiskey barrel and wanted to use it to twist their tails. The group heartily approved his scheme, and Hugh immediately proceeded to make up some signs:

THE GREAT BARREL ASCENSION!
ATTENTION — ENGINEERS!
A fig for Isaac Newton! His Law of Gravity is all wet! The architects will prove this by causing a big barrel to ascend into space from the top of White Hall at
12:00 Noon   April 17
COME ONE! COME ALL!

The architects put the signs up in the engineers' buildings: Sibley Hall and Lincoln Hall. Then they manhandled Hugh's barrel up to the top of White Hall and set it on a cornice with a black cloth over it. Below the barrel, and some distance away from the front steps, they drove stakes in the ground to hold a rope, making a fence. Everything was ready by noon the next day when a crowd of engineers started to form.

Hugh's friends lined them up behind the fence then joined hands in back of them to form a human chain. At the stroke of noon, Hugh

appeared on the roof next to the barrel. He called out, "Is everybody ready?"

"*Yaaaay!*" the engineers yelled.

"All right. Watch carefully and you'll see the barrel disappear."

With a flourish, he whipped off the black cloth, his signal to the
architects below. The human chain surged forward, packing the
engineers up against the fence.

Then Hugh kicked the barrel. It disappeared all right. It fell three
stories so fast you could hardly see it. Hitting the sidewalk, it
exploded in a shower of staves and hoops as a big geyser of water
splashed up and drenched the open-mouthed engineers.

"Can you imagine them falling for a simple trick like that?" said
Hugh afterward. "After this, I bet they won't believe everything they
read. *Now,* who's crazy?"

In their "Saloon de Garboon" on the second floor of White Hall,
architects could smoke and raise the brand of hell not appropriate
to the drafting room upstairs. "Architects' territory," it was off-
limits to outsiders. At one end of this room was an old, beat-up
piano.

Hugh redecorated this room in the Trojan style. First, he
repainted it in garish colors. Next, on the walls below the ceiling, he
painted a frieze featuring the silhouettes of his classmates, the
senior and junior architects. Then, hanging purple plush drapes
from floor to ceiling at each side of the piano, he joined them at the
top with a swag of the same material. Finally, by covering the wall
between the drapes with vertical, gilded cardboard tubes, he converted the piano into a pipe organ. How did he get away with all
that? The professors simply recognized Hugh's talents and imagination and gave him his head on such things.

Next to the Saloon de Garboon was the architects' library, sometimes used in the evening by engineering or arts students doing

"In their Saloon de Garboon, architects could smoke and raise. . . hell."   By Paul Gurney '27.

research on some special project. As the place had an offbeat reputation, they would enter rather warily. But Hugh, like his friends, considered this an invasion of their privacy. He liked to enlist his pals, Paul Gurney and Harry Wade, to help get rid of the invaders.

When an architect spotted strangers in the library, he'd run up to the drafting room and announce, "Got company, fellows."

"Hear that, Paul? Harry? Let's go!" Hugh would say.

"Okay. Lead the way," Paul would reply.

Downstairs they'd go, in their drafting room smocks. Hugh and Paul would stroll in the library and casually pretend to look over the books on the shelves. Meanwhile, Harry had run to a phone in another part of the building. From there, he'd ring the library phone. Paul would answer it.

"Library, Gurney."

"Troy? Yes, he's here. Just a minute. Here, Hugh. Wanna talk to you. About some accident."

Hugh would take the phone. "Yes, this is Hugh Troy. Yes, I have a brother. Yes, I have a Ford. Yes, he borrowed the car tonight. An *accident?* Dead? . . . My brother is . . . *dead?* I . . . I . . . Ohhhh!"

Hugh would then lose control of himself and start blubbering and moaning. Going to pieces, he'd collapse over a table. With his head buried in his arms, he'd start sobbing, loud, deep, throbbing sobs. "Oh, my brother! My poor baby brother."

Paul would try to console him. "Don't take it so hard, Hugh. There may be some mistake."

That would only make Hugh worse. Now he'd be on his back, threshing around on top of the table, yelling and flinging his arms and legs about while the saucer-eyed suckers stared, mesmerized.

"No! No!" Hugh would cry. "There's no hope. Simply *no hope!*"

With a drawn look on his face, Paul would turn to the visitors. "Lord, I don't know what in the world to do. The poor fellow's in terrible shape. I've never seen him this way before. I'd better get

"My poor baby brother . . ." By Paul Gurney '27.

some help."

Running upstairs, he'd corral their gang who were waiting for their cue. They'd clatter down the creaky old wooden stairs, hoist Hugh's six-foot-six frame to their shoulders, and carry him up the stairs, still wailing and threshing.

It always worked perfectly if they didn't do it too often. The intruders would be completely demoralized. With their research all shot to hell, they'd quickly, quietly, and respectfully slink away.

Three

As Hugh entered the spring term of 1926, he looked forward, architecture being a five-year course, to receiving his diploma in 1927. In spite of his heavy work load of studies, Hugh always found time to help many who needed him, especially freshmen. One of these was Ken Washburn who had come from California.

"When I entered Cornell," said Ken, "a greenhorn in a strange land, the first Ithacan I met was Hugh Troy. We became closely acquainted. Innocent and dependent, I leaned heavily on him. What I remember most about Hugh are not his noted achievements but his friendship, his unfailing good will, generosity, and help to a grass-green student from the Far West."

But just as Hugh extended his good will to those who needed it, he also would not silently suffer overbearing people. That spring, one of his maiden aunts, an officious, dignified dowager who had been home-bound all winter, decided to visit the Troys. Her invitation had been very tentative and the Troys were upset because she was coming just then.

She would arrive on a Friday, she said. Hugh's father and mother would be away, not returning until Saturday. But, afraid they might be considered rude, they told her they would be delighted to have her, to come anyway. They arranged with Nellie, their maid, for her care and feeding until they came home.

Hugh and his sister, Elinor, then planned a suitable reception for

Auntie. Ransacking the attic, they found some old, dilapidated furniture and placed the pieces around the house. Auntie arrived in the afternoon. Finding the accommodations delightful, she said she looked forward to staying a few days.

Sometime after dinner, Auntie corralled the afternoon paper, turned on the radio, and settled herself comfortably in Professor Troy's favorite chair in the living room. Hugh and Elinor then appeared. They had hatchets in their hands.

"Auntie," Hugh asked, "where's Nellie?"

"Why, she finished the dishes and went up to her room."

"Good," said Hugh. "Now's our chance. Elinor and I always thought there's too darned much furniture cluttering up this place. Why, you can hardly find your way through all of it. Come on, Elinor. Let's get this table."

Whack! Whack! With two hatchets flying, the table soon fell apart. Elinor picked up an armful of table pieces and carried them out. While Hugh was sailing into a rocking chair, Elinor returned. She acted horrified. "Why, Hugh! You shouldn't! That's Mother's favorite —"

Whack! Whack! "Too late now," said Hugh, as the rocker fell to pieces.

After that they invaded the dining room. But Auntie, hearing more furniture being chopped up, decided she'd had enough. She fled to her room.

In the morning, Auntie surprised Nellie by being the first one up for breakfast. "Just toast and coffee, Nellie. I've got a cab coming and have to get right back. I couldn't sleep all night worrying about my house plants. When I left I forgot to have anyone take care of them."

Hugh lavished kindness on those who deserved it. When Howard Matteson first met Hugh, Howie had just entered the architectural college. Because he was, and still is, lame, he walked with two canes. "The stairs and distances I had to walk kept me tired all the time," said Howie. "A lonesome and friendless freshman, I knew no one. I was scared that I might not be able to handle the whole damned routine."

Smiling, Hugh introduced himself to Howie, asked him a lot of friendly questions, put him at ease, and gave him confidence. "Beneath his very obvious *joie-de-vivre*," said Howie, "I sensed there lived a very gentle man. The longer I knew him, the more did I respect and admire him." Howie was impressed not only by Hugh's warm kindness and charm but also by his ability to do well anything he wanted to do, especially painting and illustration.

During his years at Cornell, Hugh was probably the best known artist there. When not painting outdoor scenes, he might be found in the coffee shop of Barnes Hall. One wall there had been marred by an ugly and prominent steam radiator. Hugh beautified the wall with a mural making the radiator the foremost element of a huge Mack truck piloted by a fat and jolly truck driver.

He also left his mark on the shelter in back of Goldwin Smith Hall where people used to wait for the trolley. After his treatment, however, it was not very popular with the fastidious, dignified set. At least they didn't care to sit on its long benches. For Hugh had painted each bench with a series of solid, black ovals, making them look like the seats in a privy.

Hugh's interest in painting and decoration developed and grew to such an extent that, in his junior year, he changed his course of studies from Architecture to Fine Arts. It led to his becoming acquainted with Ezra Winter, an artist from New York commissioned to execute the murals for Willard Straight Hall. The new student union building was a memorial to Straight, a Cornellian who had been a consul in charge of Far Eastern affairs.

Ezra Winter was a lean, brown-haired, Michigan native with a sly, dry sense of humor who, after studying in America and Italy, had gone on to become a member of many honorary societies and a fellow of the American Academy of Rome. Impressed by young Troy's ability, he engaged him to help with the lobby murals. Hugh also assisted in painting the murals in the theater. But that was only one of his many interests.

His talent could also be seen in his many drawings and cartoons published in the campus magazine, the *Widow*. Besides being on the *Widow* board, Hugh sang in the Glee Club and helped organize the annual Spring Day carnivals. That spring, in fact, he was elected chairman of the carnival committee.

With Hugh Troy in charge, the 1926 Spring Day Carnival promised to be different. It was. It became the most publicized and notorious carnival in Cornell history. Unfortunately, it disrupted the lives of many, including Hugh Troy.

That May, the *Cornell Daily Sun,* revealing Hugh's fine Irish hand, kicked off the Spring Day hullabaloo:

WORLD FLAT, SAYS BOOTHROYD
"The world is not round, but flat," asserted Cornell's noted astronomer, Professor Samuel L. Boothroyd. "I've just sent the *New York Times* startling evidence that the world is flat as a pancake. Who says the world is round? That's just fifteenth-century baloney cooked up to help Ferdinand and Isabella finance their takeover of the new world."

Students and professors took up the cry. Pinning buttons with the words, "I'M FLAT!" on their jackets, they strode the campus shouting, "Hurray for Boothroyd!" The Rounds, not to be outdone, donned hats fashioned after the tricorne worn by Columbus and sporting their slogan, "I'M ROUND!"

Professor Paul M. Lincoln then got into the act. "I'll fire a shot around the globe," he said, "to prove the world is round." Lincoln fired a cannon through the east window of Lincoln Hall but the projectile landed only three feet away from the cannon. Judges awarded Lincoln a raspberry.

Coming to the professor's rescue, Hugh apologized for Lincoln, explaining that he was only an engineer. "We Rounds invite the Flats to White Hall tomorrow to witness a real demonstration. We'll show everyone how to fire a shot around the world."

Appearing before the crowd at White Hall, Hugh stood on the steps dolled up in a long, red robe like Merlin the Magician.

"Folks," he said, "I see you have little faith in my powers. But you will change your minds when you see me *transfer a boy through space!*"

Hugh then pointed to a large wooden chest at the entrance to White Hall. "Look at this box, everyone. May I have three witnesses to examine it?"

Three fellows stepped up. Inspecting the chest, they pronounced it strong and well made.

"Now," said Hugh, "who will volunteer? Whoever comes up, we'll nail you inside the box. Then I'll concentrate on you the full force of my psychic power and pass you out of the box. Volunteers! Who will volunteer?"

"Will it hurt?" asked a towheaded youth as he stepped forward.

"Not a bit," said Hugh. "Climb right in."

The boy stepped into the container and sat down. The three witnesses nailed the cover on.

"Do you hear me?" asked Hugh as he leaned over the box.

"Ye-e-es," came a muffled reply.

Staring at the box, Hugh uttered weird sounds and waved his hands in circles. Suddenly he leaned over, pressed his ear against the cover of the chest, and called out, "Hello, are you in there?" No reply.

"Hey, let me through," shouted a boy pushing through the

crowd. He had a mop of yellow hair. The crowd burst into cheers.

"It's the same fellow!" they cried. "How'd you do it, Hugh?"

But Hugh didn't give them time to figure it out. "Now, he said, we'll fire the shot around the world." Stagehands took the box away and, at Hugh's left, set up a large screen facing the audience. An architect stood in front of the screen, holding a large metal target.

"We'll fire the shot to the east," said Hugh, brandishing an old pistol some bluecoat might have lost at Chickamauga. It had wire wound around the barrel.

"Notice that the barrel of this gun has been reinforced. We're using a special powder to give our bullet high velocity, two thousand miles a second. So, if the world is round and 25,000 miles in circumference, the bullet will return from the west in about twelve seconds and hit the mark. Keep one eye on your watch and the other on the bulls-eye."

WHOOMP! went the pistol as Hugh pulled the trigger. As the smoke drifted away, some of the spectators stared at their watches. Others stared at the target.

Twelve seconds later, BANG! Something walloped the target from the west so hard it almost flew out of the boy's hand into the crowd. The Rounds broke into cheers.

Hugh explained later how he had pulled off his tricks. "I had a fellow hidden behind the screen who shoved a long metal rod through a hole in it to wham the target. As for the boy in the box, those towheads were identical twins, the Holsman brothers from the architectural college."

The next issue of the *Cornell Daily Sun* brought a puzzled world up to date:

PARADE AND CARNIVAL TO
WELCOME COLUMBUS HOME

Starting downtown the next day, an eye-filling spectacle wound up the hill to the carnival ground under the stadium. While sidewalk vendors hawked their wares, newsboys sold copies of the *Sun*.

But then, in contrast to all this innocent fun, things took an unexpected and unpleasant turn. All along the parade route, students were guffawing at a new sheet that was giving the *Sun* competition. It was titled *The Globe and Square Dealer*. It was selling so fast that the faculty became suspicious. Some professors, however, didn't think it funny and showed it to President Farrand. His eye caught the headline on page one:

MRS. FARRAND GOES ROUND WITH DAVY HOY WHILE PRESIDENT GOES FLAT

Farrand and Davy Hoy, the registrar, might have tolerated that. But not page three:

PRESIDENT BREAKS WIND FOR NEW AERONAUTICAL COLLEGE

Amid the uproar, the faculty, with empurpled faces, demanded quick retribution. On President Farrand's order, Romeyn "Rym" Berry, manager of athletics, scurried around to all the newsstands and bought up every copy he could lay his hands on. The price then soared and the copies that Berry missed became treasured items.

To compound the commotion, the nearby *Syracuse American*, in a page-wide spread, featured photos of President and Mrs. Farrand and the front page of the scandal sheet under the page-wide headline:

"BAD TASTE" CAUSES BAN ON NAUGHTY CORNELL MAGAZINE

THE GLOBE & SQUARE DEALER

PRESIDENT BREAKS WIND FOR NEW AREONAUTICAL COLLEGE ON UPPER ALUMNI FIELD

Banquet Lends Festive Air to Occasion

After a sumptuous banquet in Willard Straight cafeteria, attended by the President and his suite, Miss Seelie, the Mesdames Woodford Flatterson, Jon English, Morris Bishwop and Reddy Smith, the party adjourned to the upper alumni field to break wind for the Upsome Areonautical College, gift to the university of the late U. R. Upsum who went down with the Shanendoah off Cape Hatterus.

In his address, Procter Twistem said, "The demand for higher education is ever growing and with this new college we should be able to compete with The University of Pittsburgh."

Captain Raoul Amundsen then gave a fine speech entitled, "How I got to Know 'em in Alaska." "Step right up and shake hands is the best way to get to Nome," exclaimed the brave commander of the, Forge, before the entire assemblage gathered at the wind breaking exercises on Hoy field. When asked if he thought the world was round or ffat he answered "Yes and No." This startling statement caused considerable excitement in the assembled crowd. One lady fainted on the spot and had to be thrown in the Tank before she came to her senses. Upon which she exclaimed, "My God, I left them scalloped potatoes in the oven all this time."

"The Globe and Square Dealer was selling so fast the faculty became suspicious."

How to find the rascals who had hurled the verbal mudballs? No problem. The masthead of the "naughty magazine" flaunted their names. Hugh Troy was properly titled, "Unmanageable Editor."

The hubbub reached such heights that Hugh thought his

'Bad Taste' Causes Ban on Naughty Cornell Magazine

BUT OTHER SHEET GOES MERRILY ON

Heavy Heel of Censor Stamps Out Quippy "Globe and Square Dealer"

Students Find Solace in "Graphic" Whose Pictured Humor Guarantees Snickers

By Staff Correspondent.

ITHACA, May 29.—You can be just a little naughty at Cornell University, but in doing it don't show "poor taste," for if you do—

That's the interpretation of the rules by students and city folks here today following the placing the ban on one student publication and failure of the college censors to frown on another, which many critics considered the "naughtier."

DENIES ANY PART.

Although the heel of the Cornell University "dictator" came down heavy to forbid further sale of "The Globe and Square Dealer," President Livingston Farrand of the University told the Sunday American reporter that he had nothing to do with the clamping down the lid on the magazine.

Another student publication, "Cornell Graphic," just check-full of "thrill" pictures, and carrying for its sub-title, "sporting numbers of the Police Gazette," was being sold like hot cakes on the campus right under the noses of the administration, but without being ordered off the news stands.

TOOK SYRACUSE TIP?

Whether Cornell officials took their tip from Syracuse University heads, who have won national "recognition" in squelching at least two "vivid" magazines recently, the Orange Peel and the Salt Shaker, could not be learned from Cornell professors.

Two references to President Farrand, president of Cornell, are said to have been the reason for the prohibition against the magazine, published in conjunction with Spring Day.

The head line to one objectionable article read:

"Mrs. Farrand Goes Round With Davy Hoy While President Goes Flat"

David Hoy is the University registrar. The name of the paper, Globe and Square Dealer, was a pun on the Spring Day dimension over the shape of the earth.

Lid on When Cornell Students Josh President Farrand

Found 1880
Burned 1926

THE GLOBE & SQUARE DEALER

MEMBER OF SATURATED CLASS

THE WEATHER
Today: Very Wet
Tomorrow: Foggy and Cloudy

Vol. 231 cu. ft., No. N-1 ITHACA, N. Y., SATURDAY, MAY 22, 1926 Price 2 Co-op Slips

"CAVE ...

MRS. FARRAND GOES ROUND WITH DAVY HOY WHILE PRESIDENT GOES FLAT

MUSIC FLAT AT NAVY HOP

Although formal announcement of the "bad taste" ban has been made, President Livingston H. Farrand denies he issued the order.

"Far Above Cayuga's Waters." That's what students captioned this picture of a young lady who has been in swimming in her street attire, and which is now under scrutiny.

Here is the offending "bad taste" headline, above, and Mrs. Farrand, wife of the Cornell President, at left, the object of the student fun-poking.

FISH EGGS AND MORE FISH EGGS

By Staff Correspondent.

WATERTOWN, May 29.—If there's no good fishing in Northern New York waters it's not because the State didn't try, for they're dumping fish eggs in numbers that look like a dozen automobile licenses placed end to end.

DIVORCEE HAS TO PAY MATE'S COURT COSTS

Justice Hits Women's Rights Resounding Thump; Makes Wifey Pay Hubby's Expense

By Staff Correspondent.

BINGHAMTON, May 29.—"Women's rights" were given a severe jolt in the granting of a divorce to Arthur M. Merriam of Binghamton by Supreme Court Justice Abraham L. Kellogg, who decreed that Mrs. Ruth Merriam, the defendant, must pay the cost of the action brought by the victorious husband.

The decree, in the opinion of those in the learned profession of the law, sets up a precedent in New York jurisprudence and promises to cause unlimited comment if it is not the basis of further court action.

SETS PRECEDENT.

It is the first time, according to members of the bar, that a woman has had to pay the cost of her husband's divorce suit. The cost of the suit is $80.75.

On top of it all Mrs. Merriam loses her dower rights the minute the decree is made final in the next 90 days.

The Merriams were married June 21, 1917. There are no children.

Named as corespondent is George A. Ogden, national guard critic. Merriam testified that with two detectives he found his wife and Ogden in her apartment early New Year's Day this year, which followed immediately after a party at a downtown hotel attended by both.

OGDEN DIVORCED.

As a sequel of the raid Ogden was recently divorced by his wife on the strength of the evidence obtained by Merriam and the two detectives.

Merriam, who still retained the key to his wife's apartment, said he walked in that early morning and found Ogden had usurped his wife's affections. His greeting was:

"Happy New Year to you," he testified.

Although the wife was in court during the trial of the suit, she did not ask for permission to testify. She was represented by an attorney.

Mother of 14 Is Sued for Divorce

NEW YORK, May 29.—Mrs. Alwine Rent, 8514 Eightieth st., Woodhaven, mother of 14 children of whom 11 are living, was yesterday for the second time in five years

The Globe and Square Dealer editorial board "before and after." Left to right, back row: W. Stewart Beecher '26, M. Birney Wright, Jr. '26, Emile J. Zimmer, Jr. '26, Norman A. Miller '26. Front row: Henry S. Lockwood, Jr. '26, Hugh Troy '26, Ransom S. Holmes, Jr. '27.

partners in crime should have a memento of their achievement. Calling them all into his uncle's studio, he had him snap their pictures in "before and after" poses.

Hugh came home with the news that he and the other culprits had been ordered to appear before the faculty committee. The Troy's neighbor, Professor Fred Barnes, happened to be there. He was a member of the committee who was more broad-minded than the others. "Pin some mistletoe to the seat of your pants," he advised Hugh. "Then, as you leave the room, flip up your coattails."

In their meeting, the faculty decided to throw them all out. But it backfired on them. After the news got out, the whole class of 1926 raised hell. Many threatened to cancel the pledges they had made to help Cornell financially after graduation. Finally the committee handed each miscreant a copy of the paper and asked him to mark every article for which he was responsible, then sign it.

Hugh's fellow-sinners suffered various fates. Some lost credit for one course, others didn't get their sheepskins until fall. Hugh, Ransom Holmes, the "Editor-and-Chef," and Henry Lockwood, the "War Correspondent," were the worst offenders — they had written the obnoxious headlines. Their penalty was harsh. In his letter to each of them, Dean William A. Hammond cancelled all their credits for that term, placed them on parole for the next term, and ordered them to leave Ithaca within five days.

His classmates admired and respected Hugh for he assumed full responsibility for the affair. That did not surprise Professor Troy who knew that Hugh always took the full blame in all his scrapes. Though his father and mother felt heavy-hearted about the outcome, they took it in stride. They thought, as did many others — including the president's wife, Daisy Farrand — that the penalties were too severe and unjustified.

Obeying Hammond's edict, Hugh, Randy, and Henry reluctantly left Cornell and stayed away until September. They came back the next term in a chastened mood. By Christmas, however, they had recovered their old zip. Hugh's New Year's card demonstrated his newfound ebullience. It represented his first satire on America's growing infatuation with greeting cards, more than covering all the holidays in the coming year, 1927.

Hugh's New Year's card

To make up his lost credits, Hugh would have had to attend classes in the following year, 1928, and was arranging to do that. But, when he heard of his classmate's plans, he changed his mind.

Four

Many of Hugh's closest friends were going to New York after graduation. Why shouldn't he go with them? After all, he was more interested in painting and decoration than in architecture. He wouldn't have his degree but he didn't need that for a career in painting. He could return later, he told himself, study for his needed credits, then get his diploma. (He never did.)

Getting in touch with his artist friend, Ezra Winter, at his studio in New York, Hugh explained the situation. Winter encouraged him to come. "I have plenty of work," he said. "Come and be my assistant until you can find jobs to handle in your own name."

What better place could an eager, talented artist choose to launch a career than in New York? The prospect was exciting. Hugh had reason to feel lucky. It was a time of easy living, a time of jobs for everyone, a time of fat pay envelopes, a time of soaring stock prices.

So that June, as Nat Owings, the Cornell architect, noted in his book, *The Spaces In Between,* "we of the class of 1927 had migrated to New York en masse with Hugh Troy as our leader. In an effort to house a substantial number of willing victims, he promptly took over a huge converted brownstone basement with an areaway on the sidewalk for direct entry."

Here, at 32 West Fifty-third Street, across the street from the Museum of Modern Art, Hugh and many of his Cornell buddies lived for a few months. Oh, yes, there was a girl there too, a shameless hussy if you were to believe the neighbors.

Because of her, the boys' apartment achieved great notoriety. The bathroom was right in back of the living room, which had a floor-to-ceiling window. When the bathroom door was open, people on the sidewalk could look right into it and see the well-endowed young lady in the nude taking a shower.

The girl was part of a mural that Hugh and his artist friends — after dining one evening on boiled cabbage and gin — had painted on the bathroom wall over the tub. She was recoiling in shock from a mouse perched on a nearby shelf, ogling her charms through a lorgnette.

If you had been a guest of Hugh's and had occasion to use the bathroom, you might not have been pleased. As you walked in and snapped on the light, you would have seen a window with cracked and broken panes. On the wall: a soggy soap dish, a rack holding dirty towels, a medicine cabinet, and in a bracket, a glass of water holding a set of false teeth. In the corner: cobwebs holding dead flies. Jagged lath and plaster jutted out of a big hole in the ceiling. It was all realistically painted, even the curtained window and a rat peeking out of a hole near the floor. The shocker, of course, was the eye-filling female painted on the wall and wearing only a startled expression.

With the light on in the bathroom, the boys would sit in the darkened living room, waiting and watching. The feet of passersby would travel past the window, stop, go back, then slowly pass again. At times, small crowds would gather as people brought their friends to gawk at the indiscreet bathing beauty.

Months later, when Hugh was moving out of the apartment, he wanted to record the mural for posterity. He borrowed a camera, set it on a tripod for a time exposure, then undressed and got in the tub. "Just then, of all times," said Hugh, "the landlady came in. With

A Heigh-Ho Club mural. "Featured were exotic deep-sea fish. . ."

her were two nice old ladies who were thinking of renting the place." He didn't have to finish the story. His listeners could easily imagine the conclusion.

Hugh was then using Ezra Winter's studio on the top floor of Grand Central Station to work on his two murals for Don "The Pirate" Dickerman's new Heigh-Ho Club on East Fifty-third Street, a fun spot for Park Avenue elite. Each mural, eight feet high by eighteen feet long, and executed in pastel shades with silver and gold leaf, depicted a scene at the bottom of the ocean. Featured were exotic deep-sea fish that Dickerman had seen when he was with the Beebe expedition to the Galapagos.

In the Heigh-Ho Club, blond, curly-haired Rudy Vallee ("My Time Is Your Time"), playing with his Connecticut Yankees, and crooning through his megaphone ("Heigh-Ho, everybody!"), made his debut and started his rise to renown. Rudy subsequently became so attached to Hugh's murals that he thought of buying them. But Dickerman wouldn't settle for less than fifteen thousand dollars.

Hugh had pressed many of his companions into service to complete the Heigh-Ho murals in time for Dickerman's opening. After they had finished, Hugh and Ezra gave a black-tie supper party for them and many mutual friends in the Grand Central Station studio, a total of over two hundred guests. At midnight, after enjoying a bountiful bar and elegant buffet, the visitors received a surprise. Hugh rolled out a huge bin full of adjustable roller skates he had rented for the occasion.

Confessing a long-repressed desire to skate over the inviting, smooth marble floors of the Grand Central Terminal, he persuaded the most daring of the group to join him. After fitting the skates to

The lower concourse, Grand Central Station, New York.

their feet, a score or more took the four elevators down to the main concourse. Over the tiled floors and ramps of the upper and lower levels they rolled as free as birds in a breeze. Hugh had posted lookouts at the entrances to the concourses to warn of possible police action.

It was a smart move. No one gave it a thought until, suddenly, through the eastern doors of the upper concourse, came a couple of astonished policemen. As the lookouts blew their whistles, the guests scrambled hurriedly into the elevators. Soaring back up to Ezra's studio, they left the bewildered bluecoats no trace of a mob of crazy roller skaters.

Beguiled by Hugh's benevolence and diverting conversation, his fellow Cornellians would often gather at his apartment. There, while entertaining them with reminiscences of old escapades, he might suggest new ones. Some of his friends might bunk there overnight if they happened to miss a ride home.

One hot summer night, Hugh invited his Cornell buddy, Norm Scott, and four other cronies to his place to enjoy some pre-Prohibition whiskey he had acquired. After bringing each other up to date on what each had been doing, Hugh remarked, "Anybody care for a little fun and games tonight?"

"Why, what have you got now?" Norm asked.

"I know an easy way we could create a hell of a traffic jam on Fifth Avenue. And nobody would ever know who did it."

His guests looked at each other.

"Risky, Hugh," said Norm. "A thing like that —" He shrugged. "We'd be caught, sure as hell."

"No, not if you — well, follow me."

Hugh then led them to the courtyard in back of his apartment where he pointed out two Consolidated Edison Company (New York's electric utility) workhorses or street barricades. From a closet he took coveralls for everyone, hard hats, three oil lamps, a pickaxe, and two shovels.

"Good Lord, Hugh," exclaimed Norm. "Where'd all this stuff come from?"

"Search me," said Hugh with a faint smile. "It just seemed to turn up here. I walked out here one day and there it was."

"Oh, I can believe that," said Norm with a straight face.

While having another drink, his friends listened to Hugh's idea and agreed on their strategy. Dressing in the work clothes, they left Hugh's place about midnight and carried the equipment to Fifth Avenue just north of Forty-fourth Street.

After setting up the barricades to block off one and a half traffic lanes, they lit the warning lamps. While cars and trucks whizzed by, Hugh expertly chalked off on the asphalt a square six feet by six feet. Taking turns with the pick and shovels, the boys started digging.

"Watch out, you guys," warned Hugh, "here comes a cop. Just keep digging."

"Good evening, officer," he said as the patrolman approached.

"Hi, ya, fellows. What's your problem?"

"Same old story," replied Hugh. "The jokers that laid the cable under here last year didn't splice it properly. Now it's leaking. We've got to dig it up and splice it right."

"Too bad. Well, if we can help in any way — Say, suppose I get my friend and handle some of this traffic for you?"

"Thanks, officer. We'd appreciate it."

While the blue coats obligingly detoured cars around the project, and an occasional police car went by, the boys shoveled away. With the hole dug, the crew left everything there, knowing the warning lamps would burn all night. Somewhat exhausted, they tramped back to Hugh's quarters where most of them turned in for the night.

The next day, Troy and his buddies inspected their excavation. Fifth Avenue was a motorist's nightmare. Infuriated police, trying to untangle the traffic snarl, kept wondering when the "workmen" would show up. Finally it dawned on them: it was all a hoax.

Did the New York Sherlocks come sniffing along the trail of the Con Ed imposters? Perhaps, for Hugh, in early 1928, deemed it an auspicious time to move. He found new quarters in a quieter

neighborhood at 8 West Seventy-sixth Street, a three-story building just a stone's throw from Central Park. Wide, winding stairs led
to his third-floor front apartment which had a bay window with a
view of the park. After living alone for a few months, he was joined
by his Cornell classmate and architect, Bob Lent.

Living so close to the park, Hugh often strolled along its shady
paths for relaxation. Sometimes, after lunch, he'd stretch out on
one of the park benches and take a nap.

On a warm spring day, one of New York's finest, let's call him

*"He found new quarters . . . at 8
West Seventy-sixth Street."*

Flanagan, saw Hugh snoozing on a bench and proceeded to acquaint him with correct park bench etiquette.

Whack! went Flanagan's club against the sole of Hugh's shoe.

"Wha . . . what's the matter, officer?" said Hugh, sitting up.

"Feet on the ground, Mac. No sleeping on the city benches."

Watching Flanagan stroll away, Hugh pondered the injustice of such a regulation. Then he smiled to himself, a very satisfied smile.

A week later, Hugh was snoozing peacefully on a bench when he got another hot-foot.

"Listen, Mac," said the lawman, "I've told you before. No sleeping on the city benches. 'Gainst the law."

"But, officer, I'm not breaking the law."

"Whaddya mean, not breaking the law?"

"Just what I said."

"Listen, Buster. You've had that bench long enough. Move along."

"No. This is *my* bench. I'm staying right here."

"*Your* bench, hey? That's the best one I ever heard. Okay. Stay right there a few minutes. We'll see what in hell's coming off here."

Ten minutes later, Flanagan and his buddy showed up with the paddy wagon. They ordered Troy into the wagon.

"Wait a minute, officer. Put the bench in too."

"*The bench?* Why?"

"Because it's *my* bench. If that doesn't go, I won't go."

Impressed by Hugh's two-hundred-pound, six-foot-six frame, the bluecoats decided to humor him and took the bench along with Hugh to the station house.

"All right," said the magistrate whom the police called "the judge." "What do we have here?"

"Your Honor," said Flanagan, "I've warned this fellow every time I caught him sleeping on a bench in the park. Today he refused to get off and —"

"Is this true, Mister . . ." The judge looked at the docket. ". . . Mr. Troy?"

"Yes, that much is true, your honor. But I —"

"Stop right there," interrupted the judge. "Officer Flanagan gave you fair warning about sleeping on public property. You've admitted it. That's enough evidence."

"But, your honor, may I say something?"

You've had your say. You admitted sleeping on a city bench."

"Oh, no, your honor. Take a look at that bench. It doesn't have the Park Department's initials on it."

"Doesn't matter. Anyone can see it's a city park bench."

"Well, then, what about *this?*" said Hugh, handing the judge a slip of paper.

The judge read it. It was a bill of sale for the bench.

Hugh had found the shop that made the benches and had bought one for himself. He and a friend had carried it into the park. Hugh had committed no crime. The judge released him. But that's not the end of the story.

Hugh realized that, because Central Park was dozens of blocks long, its various areas were patrolled by different policemen. The next day, he and his friend carried the bench a few blocks south and waited until they saw a patrolman coming. Picking up the bench, they started walking away with it.

"Hold it, boys. Where you going with that bench?"

"Why," said Hugh, "we're just taking it home."

"Oh, taking it home, are you? Well, drop it right there. I'm taking you in to the station house."

There, once again, the flabbergasted judge had to let Hugh go. And, instead of congratulating the patrolman, he dressed him down for having been taken in as a sucker.

Hugh tried it once more in another part of the park. That ended it, for the irate judge finally snapped out at Hugh, "Look Troy. This is your *last* trip in here with that blasted bench. If I ever see you with it again, I'll rip it apart and beat you over the head with the planks."

Five

Greenwich Village, to many the most interesting part of New York, fascinated Hugh. The oldest part of Manhattan, south of Fourteenth Street and east of the Hudson, it offered glamor and antiquity. Old Dutch Colonial houses with lovely doorways and fanlights graced its avenues and boulevards. Its quaint, winding streets had no monotonous gridiron plan but retained the irregular layout of New York's early Dutch settler days. It also offered Hugh a chance to mingle with kindred spirits: painters, sculptors, novelists, and playwrights. So, when Bob Lent left the Seventy-sixth Street apartment in late 1928, Hugh decided to savor the spell of the Village.

Many newcomers were settling in the popular "Back Village" near the Hudson. Here, at 11 Bank Street, Hugh found rooms. His new location was convenient to projects he was working on for Ezra Winter in the Cotton Exchange and the Cunard Building.

He should have realized that the devil-may-care attitude of many Villagers extended to their use of the telephone. He began getting wrong-number calls. At first, he'd politely correct the person calling. But, when the calls kept coming, he figured he might as well have some fun.

Many of his callers were trying to reach a bookmaker. Hugh couldn't resist the opportunity.

"Who win the fifth at Belmont?" a caller would ask.

"Belt Buckle," Hugh would reply.

"I don't get it. Sounds like you said Belt Buckle."

"I did say Belt Buckle. Belt Buckle win the fifth at Belmont. Crotch Cricket run second."

Then he would hang up, leaving the bewildered horse player trying to figure out what had happened.

The high point of Greenwich Village life, as Hugh soon found out, was the Artists' Ball, a yearly masquerade that gave Bohemians a chance to blow off steam. Deeply involved in their success, Hugh's enthusiasm led him, at one such affair, to turn up as a shower bath. A vertical rod strapped to his back held a large ring over his head from which hung a shower curtain. He'd dance up to a damsel, part the curtain and whisk her inside, then glide away in complete privacy.

As his digs on Bank Street were near Sheridan Square and Loew's Sheridan Theater, Hugh often took in the movies. Preferring to sit in the balcony, he once took a seat right in front of the projection booth. Being so tall, every time he stood up to admit newcomers his head interfered with the projection beam.

With the picture distorted, the audience howled, bringing the manager on the double. Instead of quietly talking to Hugh, he anointed him with a torrent of impolite language, to the great amusement of those sitting nearby. Hugh didn't say a word. But on his next trip to the Sheridan he settled the score.

With him was his old comrade, Bob Alexander, who noticed that Hugh was carrying a small cardboard box tied with string.

"What's in the box?" Bob asked.

"Oh, nothing special," Hugh replied. "I'll show you when we get to the movies."

After they sat down, Hugh put the box on the floor. They had seen about half the show, a Greta Garbo film, when Bob saw Hugh reach for the box.

"Watch this, Bob," Hugh whispered.

Untying the string, he took the cover off the box. Out flew a cloud of giant moths. They all zeroed in on the projection beam. What a scenic effect on the screen! It was devastating, a fantastic light show!

Soon the projector stopped. The house lights came on. Up the stairs bounded the manager, swatting at the moths with a broom. But most of them had swooped down to frolic around the chandelier. Thinking they might stay there, the boss turned out the house lights and started the projector. Back into the beam flew the flutterbugs, again covering the screen with their dancing shadows.

After a hurried discussion with the projectionist, the manager gave up. He called off the show and passed out "moth-checks" for a future performance.

In October of the following year, 1929, America, reeling from the greatest stock market crash in history, plunged into depression and gloom. Bank after bank, business after business, closed their doors. Bread lines were common, jobs scarce. With over ten million out of work, unemployed executives were reduced to selling apples on street corners. In truth, the depths to which America had fallen became the theme of a popular song, "Buddy, Can You Spare A Dime?"

Among the thousands losing their jobs were many of Hugh's friends. But Hugh was fortunate. As he had a number of contracts to paint murals, agreements he had made before hard times struck, he had a good income. So good, in fact, that in early 1930, he left Bank Street for a better location.

His attractive new studio was on Minetta Lane, a picturesque old street only one block long and one block south of Washington Square in the heart of the Village. "Gentleman Jim" Walker, New York's mayor, lived nearby while ex-governor Al Smith resided across the Square in a large apartment house at One Fifth Avenue.

As Hugh was moving in he sent his acquaintances a change-of-address notice. Fifteen by thirty inches, it was a take-off on the

Subway Sun that the Metropolitan Transit Authority posted in all its trains:

SUBWAY SUN

ONE OF OUR PATRONS OF LONG STANDING, A MR. HUGH TROY, WHO MOVED FROM 11 BANK ST. TO 16 MINETTA LANE, WAS HEARD TO REMARK, AS HE WAS SHOVED OFF A FLATBUSH AVENUE EXPRESS: "HAPPY NEW YEAR EVERYONE. THERE'S PLENTY OF ROOM ON THE EL."

That Easter Hugh invited his friends to a housewarming. It featured an egg-dying contest. When the eggs were all dyed, Hugh ran out into the street, grabbed the first three kids he could find, and had them act as a jury to select the prettiest egg. To the winner, he awarded a box of Easter candy. The runner-up got a toy rabbit in which Hugh had stuffed a hard-boiled egg to make it appear pregnant.

Learning that his fellow-artist, Erling Brauner, had just left Cornell for New York, Hugh invited him to share his Minetta Lane lodging for a while. A gracious gesture, it derived from Hugh's desire to ease Erling's way into life in the big city.

Dutifully escorting his friend around the metropolis, Hugh introduced him to Ezra Winter and many other painters. These included muralist "Put" Brinley with whom Hugh was then decorating the spectacular globe of the world, twelve feet in diameter, that revolves in the lobby of the *Daily News* building on East Forty-second Street. Hugh's contribution to the globe included, near the South Pole, the "Troy Islands." As he explained to a startled visitor, "I really don't know if there are any islands there, but if there are, then that's their name."

*The apartment house at
16 Minetta Lane*

Because of the depression, many of the artists Hugh and Erling visited were out of work and, in those days before welfare and food stamps, had no idea where their next bag of groceries might come from. "I then became," said Erling, "an involuntary witness to Hugh's compassion and limitless generosity. No one ever knew how many meals he bought for his unfortunate friends. He just quietly gave."

"I wasn't surprised to hear that," said Hugh's brother, Fran, who was to share an apartment with him later. "When we roomed together, he was always giving his things away. If he couldn't find something of his own, he'd give my things away."

Erling's fondest memories of Hugh center not so much around his keen sense of humor as around his wonderfully gentle and kind disposition. "In the years I knew him," said Erling, "from the mid-twenties to the mid-thirties, I never knew Hugh to utter an unkind remark about anyone regardless of what his personal feelings might be. This is not to suggest that Hugh was in any way insensitive to variations in human behavior. On the contrary, he was extremely perceptive of human beings and their motives." In spite of that perceptiveness, Hugh had a great tolerance for the foibles of mankind as shown by one of his favorite remarks: "It is so easy to make

". . . Hugh (top) was then decorating the spectacular globe of the world . . ."

a friend, I cannot understand making an enemy."

Hugh loved his third floor walk-up on Minetta Lane because it was a veritable slice of Paris. To reach it he had to unlock an iron gate at the street, walk through a passageway to a rear courtyard, then climb two flights of stairs. These led to his studio, about twenty by thirty-five feet, with a tremendous skylight over a large drawing table where he worked. Also in the room were his celebrated park bench, chairs, bookcases, and a couple of beds. A combined kitchen and dining area came in handy for anyone with a yen to cook. Hugh took advantage of his new quarters, commodious by Village standards, to entertain dozens of his friends.

Instinctively gregarious, Hugh had a boundless hospitality, and was known as a supreme spinner of titillating tales. Largely his own adventures in deception, those tales revealed his Irish gift for beautifying truth for the unimaginative, for imparting an extraordinary quality to the events of everyday life. With all this, Hugh was also self-effacing, easygoing, with a humility bordering on diffidence. Such a reputation attracted friends and strangers alike. They were drawn, like bees to a buttercup, to 16 Minetta Lane.

Some of his visitors, as his next roommate, Cornell engineer and fraternity brother Karl Kellerman, recalls, had more on their minds than just paying a social call. In those days of bread lines, soup kitchens, hobo camps, and bonus marchers, many were looking for a place to stay "just a few nights," as they'd put it, until they could find a job. "Hugh wouldn't dream of turning them away," said Karl. "If there was no bed for them, he'd let them sleep in chairs or on the floor."

As news of Hugh's generosity spread, his visitors hit such peaks on weekends that it was hard for anyone to walk across the floor during the night without stepping on someone. What bothered Hugh most though was that he and Karl slept in comfort in their twin beds while those staying the night roughed it on the hard floor.

"So he bought two more mattresses and springs," said Karl. "Adding the springs from our beds to the two new ones, he laid them all on the floor one way and placed the mattresses across them the other way. This made a huge harem-type affair about seven by fourteen feet. A sailmaker named Ratsey, who had outfitted many America Cup winners, stitched up some special sheets to fit our new arrangement.

"On this bed, as big as a trampoline, Hugh and I and our guests for the night, up to five or six, slept side by side, partly clothed, sometimes slightly inebriated, but never indecent. Occasionally, in the darkness, a few groans and grumbles might be heard when some befuddled wine-bibber tried to crawl into bed without noticing that someone else had preempted the space he was heading for."

The Bowery-type sleeping conditions eventually resulted in a nickname for Hugh's quarters. Many of his guests attended boxing matches at Boyle's Thirty Acres in Jersey City where the benches were so close together that the spectators almost sat in each other's laps. Marvelling at the crawling masses of humanity at Boyle's, Hugh's friends drew the obvious parallel and christened the artist's place, "Troy's Thirty Acres."

Many a Cornellian, on his return to Ithaca after visiting the big city would be asked, "And where did you stay in New York?"

"Why, Troy's Thirty Acres," he'd reply. "Where else?"

Many of Hugh's canvases took up so much floor space at Minetta Lane that, by the summer of 1931, he was searching for a larger studio. He finally found a spacious room over Manny Wolfe's Chop House, a restaurant on the northeast corner of Third Avenue and East Forty-ninth Street that was Rudy Vallee's favorite hangout.

For fifty dollars a month, Hugh also rented an apartment nearby at 151 East Forty-ninth, a room and a half with bath on the fifth floor of a five-floor brick walk-up. Hugh's Cornell friend, Frank Sullivan, the New Yorker's peerless humorist, lived with Corey Ford nearby

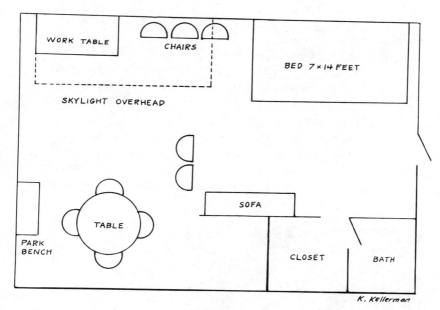

"Troy's Thirty Acres."

on East Fifty-first.

"It was a friendly neighborhood," wrote Sullivan, "as sequestered as if it were a hundred miles from Broadway." Katharine Cornell, James Forrestal, and Lillian and Dorothy Gish lived in an apartment east of Sullivan's. For most of the next ten years, Hugh shared his quarters with his brother, Fran, an accounting executive, who replaced Hugh's first roommate, Jack Powell, a writer with Time magazine and gleeful recorder of Trojan capers.

Soon after he had his phone connected, Hugh again began getting wrong-number calls. By that time though he had perfected his methods of handling them. His new number happened to differ by only one digit from the number for the nearby Baldwin's Fish

Market. Here, via tape, is Hugh's story of how he would handle his orders for fish.

Now, this was not premeditated at all, but I'd be there, having probably worked until three or four in the morning. The phone would ring about seven o'clock. It might be a fellow that wanted some haddock. I'd say, "Well, that'll be eighty-five dollars a pound."

"Well, ah," he'd say, "that seems rather odd to me. I think I got some from you last week for, ah, forty cents."

"Well," I'd say, "I must tell you something mister. There's an embargo on haddock right now. And we

"He rented an apartment at 151 East Forty-ninth . . ."

happen to have the only three pounds in New York. Tell you what. I'll let you have two pounds of haddock for a hundred and forty dollars."

Slam! went the phone.

A few minutes later it would ring again and some lady might say, "I'd like some cod, but I want it very fresh."

I'd try to tell her she had the wrong number but at that hour in the morning you couldn't argue with her. So I'd say, "Madam, if you want fresh codfish, the cod that you're going to eat tonight is still swimming in the Atlantic. We've got radio control on our boats and I'm telling you that I'll get in touch with them right now. You just tell me what time you need it to pop in the oven and you'll have it."

So she'd give me her order and I'd spend a few hours drawing a big, fantastic codfish on a block of wood. Then, toward the end of the day, I'd wrap it up and deliver it to her Park Avenue address just in time for her to pop it in the oven.

While Hugh was getting settled down, John D. Rockefeller, Jr. was breaking ground on Fiftieth Street near Fifth Avenue for the world's largest privately owned business and entertainment complex, Rockefeller Center, a project that was to fill three city blocks.

Watching the activity through a flimsy picket fence around the pit was a favorite noontime diversion of hundreds of curious persons including Hugh and his friend, Alice Woodward, secretary to Rockefeller's public relations director, Merrill Crowell.

"John D. plans to put up a strong, high board fence to keep people back from that pit," Alice remarked to Hugh.

"Then how can everyone watch what's going on?" asked Hugh.

"Guess they'll be out of luck," replied Alice.

The next day Hugh passed a note to Rockefeller: "People like to watch your building going up. Why not cut a series of portholes in your new fence so they can watch the work going on?" Delighted with Hugh's suggestion, Rockefeller ordered the holes cut and, after the fence was built, hundreds of New Yorkers followed the building's progress in safety through the portholes.

Hugh thanked Rockefeller in a unique way. Nearly every noon, walking along the fence, Hugh handed each spectator a card he had designed and had printed.

"𝕯𝕖 𝕓𝕖𝕤𝕥𝕖 𝕤𝕥𝕦𝕦𝕣𝕝𝕦𝕚 𝕤𝕥𝕒𝕒𝕟 𝕒𝕒𝕟 𝕨𝕒𝕝"
(The best pilots stand on the shore)

THE SIDEWALK SUPERINTENDENTS' CLUB
Rockefeller Center
welcomes you as a charter member, and extends the privileges and courtesies of the Club to the bearer of this card.

Hugh's design on the card was a coat of arms showing an All-Seeing Eye, a windmill in a tulip field, a storm at sea, a pickaxe shattering the face of a clock, and a power shovel biting the earth. This was supposed to represent the Dutch (Rockefellers) braving the ocean crossing to sail to America then laboring long hours to build Manhattan.

Rockefeller liked Hugh's card so much that he too would walk around his project handing them out. "The idea of the portholes was hailed by newspapers with delight," wrote Raymond B. Fosdick, Rockefeller's biographer, "a great benefaction to mankind." Soon contractors in other states followed suit and sawed similar holes in their fences. Hugh's term, "sidewalk superintendent," became part of our language and now appears in most American dictionaries.

Six

Attracted by Hugh's charisma and his ability as a story teller many Cornell and New York friends became fellow residents at 151 East Forty-ninth Street. They enjoyed Hugh's flair for the felicitous phrase, his keen relishing of the absurd and ridiculous. With becoming modesty, and in a low-key, gentle, unforced manner, he would regale his listeners for hours with memories of his deceptions and proposals for droll new projects. One of his deceptions grew out of the sales efforts of the local speakeasies.

Hugh and his fellow-tenants at 151 purchased their potables at either a Third Avenue drugstore or a nearby soda parlor. Trying to corral the market, the two merchants competed in a goldfish promotion. Buy two quarts of liquor and get a small bowl or a goldfish free; buy three quarts and get a large bowl or three fish, and so on.

Hugh's guests soon became used to seeing his bowl of fish near his favorite chair. But they weren't prepared to see him eat them. After dinner with a visitor, he might flop into his chair and light a cigarette. As was his custom, if an ashtray wasn't handy, he'd tap the ashes into his pants cuff. Then, murmuring something about being "still a little hungry," he'd reach into the bowl and grab a golden morsel. Suspending it by its tail, he'd drop it into his mouth and chew it down while carrying on his conversation. As he later told a friend, "My 'fish' was an imitation I had made from a carrot."

For dinner, the artist would sometimes serve oysters on the half-shell. "Oh, look, Hugh," a guest would exclaim, holding up a large pearl.

". . . he might flop into his chair and light a cigarette."

"Gee! Congratulations! Some people have all the luck."

Rushing breathlessly into a jewelry store the next day, the treasure-finder would say, "I just found this beautiful pearl. Would you please appraise it for me?"

"Why," the jeweler would snort after inspecting it, "you're the second fellow's come in here with one of them ten-cent-store pearls."

In the basement of Hugh's apartment house was a speakeasy called the Pilots' Club run by a fellow called "Laughing Jack." The owner, who lived on the first floor, was a Captain Hallahan who had retired from the New York Police Department. He rented the whole building to Laughing Jack, whose operation was thereby endowed with a permanence envied by his competitors.

Running out of work for a spell that fall, and unable to pay his rent, Hugh had to give Laughing Jack some IOU's. After holding them fretfully a few months, Jack cagily decided his barroom needed a new decorating job and commissioned Hugh to do the work. Hugh thereupon enlisted a team of fellow artists to help him, including Dr. Seuss (Ted Geisel) and cartoonist Abner Dean.

"Listen, fellows," Hugh told them, "before we start, let's all agree on one thing: no one is to follow his own style." The result was a blend of Hugh Troy by Abner Dean, Abner Dean by Dr. Seuss, and Dr. Seuss by Hugh Troy.

What Laughing Jack got was insanity run riot: a gallimaufry of bizarre beasts, snakes slithering around exposed plumbing, and brazen belly-dancers bumping and grinding in every corner. Although the artists were proud of the results, the boss gave the scenes the fisheye. Some of the wanton women, he grumbled, flaunted too many charms, even for a speakeasy.

"Hugh," he said with a frown, "you'll have to tone 'em down." So Hugh and his team painted black lace skimpies over the most blatant vulgarities. Jack was still dubious.

But startled customers soon spread the news of the artwork by word of mouth, accompanied by raised eyebrows and low whistles. Soon the Pilots' Club became a popular watering hole. Realizing he'd made a fine investment, Laughing Jack tore up Hugh's chits and treated his team to drinks and a full-course spaghetti dinner.

"People should be mystified more than they are," Hugh once asserted. "Life moves along too regularly." On his trips by subway, he would often use his great height to demonstrate that belief. In Hugh's day, the fare, believe it or not, was five cents.

Hugh would enter a subway station with a friend during a rush hour when a long line of commuters was waiting at the change booth. After running his hands through his pockets, he would remark, "Gosh, I don't have any nickels."

His companion, after a similar search, would often say, "Gee, neither do I. I'll go and get some." Whipping a bill from his wallet, he'd head for the line at the change booth. Ideally, for Hugh's purpose, their train would then come roaring in.

"No, wait!" Hugh would exclaim. "Put your money away. I think I can find some." Reaching up to a beam over eight feet above the floor, he'd pick off a couple of nickels. Thrusting one into the hand of his wide-eyed companion, he'd say, "Here! Let's go. This trip's on me."

For such coin "discoveries," Hugh had stashed away nickels and dimes not only in his favorite subway stations but also on high ledges near bus stops and in the fretwork over the train platform entrances in Grand Central Station.

Any projection on the front of a building would serve as his temporary bank. Here Hugh himself recounts another hidden coin incident:

> On the front of a building on Fifth Avenue was a sign saying, "Hanscom's Bake Shop" with letters made of stainless steel that were within my reach. When I was walking by there one night with a girl named Virginia, I left a quarter in the bottom of the "O" of that sign. "Virginia," I said, "I know you can't reach it but you'll know it's there."
>
> One of our friends named Frank was nearly as tall as I was and later, when Virginia was walking by there with him, she gave it away.
>
> "Frank," she said, "the other night Hugh put a quarter up there in the bottom of that 'O'. Let's fool him and change it." So Frank took the quarter and left a nickel and two dimes.
>
> But Virginia couldn't hold her tongue and told me about it. "Frank doesn't know I'm telling you this," she said, "but the other night he and I were walking by the bake shop and he left change for your quarter."
>
> Now this all happened just before we went off the gold standard so I was able to buy a ten-dollar gold piece which is just about the size of a dime. I then walked into

the drugstore where Frank always ate lunch.

"Frank," I said, as I showed the gold piece to him, "the strangest thing happened to me. I was out with Virginia the other night and left a quarter in the 'O' of the Hanscom's sign. Well, I needed it tonight so I reached up for it. You know what? Someone had changed it and left me a nickel, a dime, and this ten-dollar gold piece."

If you had peeked out the rear window of Hugh's apartment at 151, you would have glimpsed a dreary vista of backyards, washing hanging from clotheslines, trash piles, and garbage cans. By shifting your eyes a bit, however, you would have seen a more intriguing view. For, to cheer up his place, Hugh had covered two facing walls with a mural showing the skyline of New York. By assuming a high point of view, he gave you the illusion that you were looking over the city from the top of a tall building. The drawing was realistic enough to induce vertigo.

Still more intriguing was a peculiarly appropriate mural that covered all four walls of his bathroom. He had painted this in black and white on a gold leaf background in the Persian manner, without perspective. Royal Persians on a holiday or fiesta were disporting themselves in a garden setting amid flowers, pools, and fountains. They were picnicking and playing games, with a polo game in the foreground. Near the polo grounds, inside a small tent with its flaps open, the king squatted on a portable "throne," answering nature's call while intently watching the game.

Flying from a pole at the top of the tent was a small banner carefully lettered in flowing script. After searching all over New York, Hugh had finally found a Persian fruit merchant who could draw the Persian inscription: MEN. He had located the royal tent so that you would not see it until you had entered the bathroom, closed the door, and seated yourself. You could then view in comfort and empathy this intimate slice of Persian life.

Hugh's bathroom art attracted so much attention that the artist sensed its money-making possibilities and decided to promote it more vigorously. Calling on one of his friends, Margaret Fishback, whose poems often appeared in the *New Yorker,* he persuaded her to write some verse for him. He then sent it to his prospects on postcards:

> To keep the wolf outside my door,
> I'll do a batch of murals for
> Your bathroom. Cows or sheep or ducks
> Will cost you just one hundred bucks.
>
> So let me then infest your walls
> With Venice or Niagara Falls
> Or nature studies if you wish
> Except I draw the line at fish.

His first customer was the "park bench statesman," international financier, and adviser to presidents, Bernard Baruch, who had headed President Wilson's War Industries Board. "Hugh," said Baruch, "we'll be in Europe for a few weeks this summer. Why don't you just move in to my place while you're working? The servants will take care of you." Hugh agreed and lived in Baruch's posh apartment at 4 East Sixty-sixth Street while painting an elaborate mural in his bathroom.

Other customers followed. For another client's powder room, Hugh painted a melange of beautiful, pink dancing pigs. This was followed by a mural for Louis Seagrave, president of United Founders Corporation, who was opening a spacious apartment in a high-rise co-op at One Beekman Place. Decorating Seagrave's forty-foot-long entrance hall with a grandiose Venetian canal scene, he populated it with gondolas propelled by likenesses of his friends.

As Christmas of 1931 approached, merchants trotted out their usual displays of greetings. Hugh, however, detested the common run-of-the-rack Christmas cards. "For years," he complained, "I've been getting fed up with the cards people send me. They show pictures of cocktail shakers, polar bears, Dutch windmills, any damned thing that has nothing to do with Christmas." Satirically, he decided that if his friends took such liberties with him, he'd send them cards they would remember.

In a stationery store, he bought a supply of paper with a faint design of meandering lines. He had it cut Christmas-card style and printed with only a border and this message:

SOAK THIS CARD IN TEPID WATER FIVE MINUTES
HUGH TROY

The scores of friends who received his cards would try warmish water but no design or message would appear. So they'd figure they'd used water too warm or too cold and would try again. They'd try and try. Only after their card came apart in soggy fragments would they realize they'd been had.

Many wrote him that their cards must have been defective because they had soaked them for hours on end. Others called him, saying, "Why, Hugh, Santa's head appeared but what about the rest of him?"

The response Hugh liked best was a wire he received from F. Chase Taylor, known as the radio comedian, Lemuel Q. Stoopnagle. Arriving in Western Union's gay green-and-red, holly-berry Christmas envelope, it read:

GO SOAK YOUR HEAD

In the depression year of 1932, business firms were cutting corners. Decorating work, something that could be deferred, was hard to get, even for an artist with a national reputation such as Ezra Winter. Hugh was ingenious, though, and helped Ezra find ways to underbid competitors and keep bread money rolling in.

Ezra planned, for instance, on redecorating a large church with a long gallery and a vaulted ceiling between the sanctuary and chapel. After surveying the building carefully, Hugh suggested to Ezra a unique way to cut the cost of the job. "Good thinking, Hugh," said Ezra. "We'll bid it that way."

Two other artists submitted their bids, including the cost of erecting and taking down scaffolds they would need to reach the high places. The bids were opened. Ezra's figure was far below the others. "How could he possibly do it so cheaply?" the losers asked one another.

They found out when they saw Hugh in action. With extension handles tied to his brushes to augment his six-foot-six-inch height, he was easily painting the high places without the aid of scaffolds.

John D. Rockefeller, Jr.'s project, now partially completed, also brought needed employment for them. Hugh helped Ezra paint the sixty-by-forty foot "Fountain of Youth" mural in the Grand Foyer of Radio City Music Hall, the world's largest indoor theater. So huge that Ezra and Hugh had to paint it in an unused tennis court, the landscape portrays an Oregon Indian legend of the beginning of time when the world was new.

A mountain top, separated by a deep chasm from a rocky promontory in the foreground, is shown gleaming in a golden light.

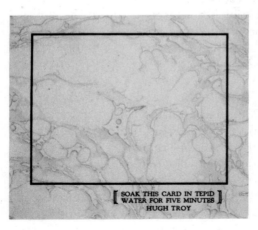

Hugh's Christmas card

The "Fountain of Youth" mural, Radio City Music Hall, New York.

An old man, who has followed the path of the ages in search of the fountain of youth, stands in the foreground gazing at the mountain, realizing the impossibility of ever reaching it. Passing before him is a rainbow procession of the ambitions and vanities of his life. The panorama so pleased Rockefeller that words failed him.

Hugh's next enterprise grew out of one of his frequent trips to Ithaca to see his parents. The project, which greatly increased his reputation but not the thickness of his wallet, was the decorating of Cornell's Barton Hall for the 1933 Junior Prom. Hugh conceived an Alice In Wonderland theme with an effect more dramatically lovely than those the Ecole des Beaux Arts created for their annual balls in Paris.

Working with the committee, Hugh covered with cloth the perimeter and ceiling of the large dance area to create a tremendous enclosed space of midnight blue. At one end he applied a huge figure of a rabbit holding a hat, at the other, Alice. Each figure stood some thirty feet high. Out of the rabbit's hat flew a stream of giant cards clear to the ceiling, the cards gradually increasing in size until those near the ceiling were some ten feet long.

While in Ithaca, Hugh also executed a mural for the Great Hall of his fraternity, Delta Upsilon. Painted in striking colors, the formalized landscape extended from floor to ceiling. Another mural, in the bar, featured fantastic animals, a la Dr. Seuss. A six-inch pipe crossed over the bar a foot below the ceiling and the tail of one of the creatures left the wall and wrapped around the pipe. Lurking in other parts of the room were three or four other savage beasts. It was claimed by the fraternity brothers that the whole scene greatly magnified the effect of even one glass of beer.

Back in New York in the fall of 1934, Hugh executed the striking murals in the new Cafe Lounge of Manhattan's Savoy Plaza Hotel where tea dancing was enjoyed during the cocktail hours. His paintings, each eight feet high by fourteen feet long, on three walls of the room, depicted horses and carriages with men and women wearing top hats and hoop skirts amidst nostalgic ante-bellum backgrounds. During the gala opening of the new lounge — the Savoy's announcements featured "original murals by Hugh Troy" — hundreds of guests admired the paintings.

Among them was Clare Boothe Luce, wife of Henry Luce (publisher of Time, Life, Fortune), who invited Hugh and his Cornell architect friend, Art Odell, to a dinner-dance. For such parties in that big-band era it was often a question whether to wear a black tie or white tie and tails.

"What'll we wear, Hugh?" asked Art.

"Oh, black tie will be okay."

They arrived at the party to find that they were the only ones not in white tie and tails. Mrs. Luce spied Hugh. "Oh, dear, Hugh. I owe you an apology."

"You do? Why?"

"I've embarrassed you. I didn't think of mentioning what to wear."

"Oh, think nothing of it, Clare. Of course I knew everyone would be wearing white tie and tails and planned on wearing mine tonight, but I had an accident. You see, I came home from a party last night in my best clothes. Without thinking, I picked up my brushes and finished a painting I had started. Darned if I didn't spatter paint on my tails. Now they're at the cleaner's. So I came this way rather than miss your party."

"Oh, what a shame, Hugh. Sure, we understand. It's easy to see

A portion of Hugh's mural in the former Savoy Plaza Hotel, New York.

how that could happen."

"Mrs. Luce and her guests laughed at the humorous way Hugh explained his predicament," said Art. "It let him off the hook very nicely. But it left me with egg on my face and the feeling that I was the only rube on hand."

"Sorry about that, Art," said Hugh afterward. "I made up the first excuse that came into my head. I don't really have any tails. They're too damned much trouble."

Some months later, New York's Museum of Modern Art scheduled America's first Van Gogh exhibition. When it opened, in 1935, Hugh was one of the first ones there. He later said he might just as well have stayed home.

The exhibit attracted so many people the crush was unbelievable. No one could get a decent look at the paintings. Hugh suspected that most of the spectators were attracted by Van Gogh's reputation — particularly the tale of how he sliced off one of his ears and sent it to his favorite prostitute — than by his work. He thought of a way to test his theory.

Carving an ear out of a hunk of dried beef, he mounted it professionally in a velvet-lined shadow box. Below he fastened a sign:

THIS IS THE EAR THAT VAN GOGH CUT OFF
AND SENT TO HIS MISTRESS DEC. 24, 1888

Smuggling it into the museum, he hung it on the wall. His theory was vindicated. Most of the crowd was drawn, gawking and open-mouthed, to the "ear" leaving plenty of space for Hugh to stroll about and enjoy Van Gogh's work at his leisure.

"Van Gogh's Ear," as pictured by Tom Wolfe

Seven

A girl friend once visited Hugh and was surprised to see a bone about eighteen inches long lying on an end table. She asked him about it.

Hugh gave her about the same yarn he later told others. Every time he repeated a story, he would add more hors d'oeuvres, spice, and garnish to the original meat-and-potatoes version so that it eventually became a feast for the imagination.

According to Hugh, he had been home for a couple of weeks in the fall of 1936. While there, he was painting murals in the Connecticut Yankee Lounge of the Mark Twain Hotel in nearby Elmira where Twain lived for nearly forty years. (The paintings, on two walls of the lounge, represented scenes from the author's book, *A Connecticut Yankee In King Arthur's Court.*)

As December approached, Hugh's mother, then an invalid, asked him, "Hugh, dear, what would you like for Christmas?"

"Gee, Mother, I haven't thought about it yet."

"Well, to make it easy for me why don't you just get what you want and I'll pay you for it?"

"All right, Mother. I understand."

Over a week went by while Hugh pondered what his Christmas present would be. A few days later, an article in the *Ithaca Journal* told how road builders had unearthed a female skeleton near the neighboring town of Van Etten. Not being able to trace its history, they were uncertain what to do with it.

One of Hugh's murals in the former Connecticut Yankee Lounge of the Mark Twain Hotel, Elmira, N.Y.

Hugh said later he made a quick trip to the site where he wangled the bones to study anatomy. Many artists, of course, are interested in that. The author and illustrator, Lewis Carroll, owned a "set of bones." The painter, Thomas Eakins, who made a hobby of dissection, was obsessed with anatomy.

As it turned out, Hugh did acquire the bones and brought his unique Christmas present home. It took his mother a while to get over her shock. But, as the days went by, her feelings gradually changed to tolerance, then to amusement. She alluded to it later.

"Hugh packed the bones in a suitcase," said Mrs. Troy, "and took them with him to New York on the Lehigh Valley Railroad. When the train was pulling into Manhattan, a porter came into the car to help Hugh carry his bags to the door. 'Just a minute,' said Hugh as he took the suitcase down from the rack and laid it on a seat. 'I have to check something.' He opened the case and the porter suddenly vanished."

In New York, Hugh wired the lady's bones together and kept her in a box. Later, at a party in his apartment, he took the skeleton out to show his friends. It drew so much attention that he took it out to a few other parties to liven things up a bit.

At those affairs, a friend would ask him, "Ye gods, Hugh, what have you got there?"

"Oh, hello. I want you to meet my grandmother."

"Your grandmother? What in the world is she doing here?"

"Well, she turned up when they moved a road in the cemetery where she was buried. I thought she should have one last fling before we buried her again. Don't you think she deserves it?"

Then someone tipped off the gossip columnist and newscaster, Walter Winchell. When he heard how Miss Slenderella was clattering around to various shindigs, he mentioned it in his Sunday night radio broadcast.

Hugh's Aunt Rose heard the broadcast while on a ship sailing from Miami to Cuba and didn't believe her ears. She couldn't wait to get to Havana. At six the next morning in Ithaca, N.Y., Professor Troy, roused from a sound sleep, answered his doorbell. As he opened his door, a young man handed him this:

PATRONS ARE REQUESTED TO FAVOR THE COMPANY BY CRITICISM AND SUGGESTION CONCERNING ITS SERVICE

1201B

CLASS OF SERVICE		SIGNS
This is a full-rate Telegram or Cable-gram unless its de-ferred character is in-dicated by a suitable sign above or preced-ing the address.	**WESTERN UNION**	DL = Day Letter
		NM = Night Message
		NL = Night Letter
		LCO = Deferred Cable
		NLT = Cable Night Letter
	NEWCOMB CARLTON, PRESIDENT J. C. WILLEVER, FIRST VICE-PRESIDENT	WLT = Week-End Letter

The filing time as shown in the date line on full-rate telegrams and day letters, and the time of receipt at destination as shown on all messages, is STANDARD TIME.

Received at 105 South Aurora St., Ithaca, N. Y.

HAVANA CUBA   MAY 17, 1937

URGENT

PROFESSOR HUGH TROY   ITHACA NEW YORK

WHAT IS HUGH DOING WITH MOTHER'S SKELETON?

IS HE TAKING IT TO PARTIES?

ROSE

About that time, Hugh, who would go to any lengths to embarrass a friend, found himself on the wrong end of the joke. The artist had a pal, Harry Klug, who he had tricked in some way. Some time after that, Harry called Hugh up.

"Say, Hugh, Alice and I are having a little dinner party at our place next Saturday evening and would like very much to have you attend. Think you can make it?"

"Gee, thanks a lot, Harry. Sure, Saturday sounds fine. Glad to come."

"Good. Say, by the way, Hugh, would mind stopping along the way to pick up Minnie Lovelace? She was Alice's maid of honor at our wedding."

"Oh, no trouble at all, Harry."

On the way to the party Hugh stopped at the address and sent up his name. The lady came down. Hugh gazed down at her from his six-foot-six height. She was exactly thirty-nine inches tall. Harry had arranged for her to entertain guests at the party with recollections of her circus days and had used the opportunity to give Hugh a taste of his own practical-joker medicine.

Hugh couldn't wait to pay Harry back. But he couldn't find a good chance to work it out. Time dragged along. It looked as though Harry had won that round because he was sailing for Europe on business in a few days.

Sailing time came. At the steamer, Hugh was on hand with other friends to say good-by. Meek and quiet, he offered no tricks. He left before the others. After the "All ashore!" gong, Harry, tired, and not sorry to be alone, went to his stateroom. (It was a double-berth room but he thought he would have it alone.)

Damnation! The ship was crowded. A roommate!

Inside the door hung a greasy old checked suit. It stank. The room was repulsive with the odors of a grimy shirt, soiled underwear, and limp, ancient socks on the floor. In the washbasin were two used cornplasters. An indelicate photograph was stuck in the mirror.

In the other berth was a broken-handled rattan suitcase. The fellow had evidently changed his clothes after coming aboard.

Harry couldn't get through the crowd in the purser's office. He spent the night in a half-doze in the smoking room rather than sleep with that crumb.

Next morning he noticed the suitcase hadn't been moved. He shoved it to one side. Under it was a note:

> Dear Harry
> Have a great trip.
>   Hugh

That summer, fancying herself a patron of the arts, a rich and famous lady planned a benefit carnival and art auction at her estate at Sands Point, Long Island. Her affair was strictly by invitation, the only people to attend being the cream of the social register crowd. Commanding various artists, including Hugh, to volunteer their services, she asked them to bring their paints and brushes.

Arriving at her mansion, they were escorted into her lordly presence. "I'm giving you just two minutes of my time," she told them imperiously. "Your task is very simple. Each of you is to paint a picture for the auction. You'll find easels and various sizes of canvases and illustration board on the terrace. You may leave your paintings right there. Please get to work right now. My carnival starts in two hours."

"Will we be attending your carnival?" timidly asked one of the painters.

"Oh, no. Our caterers have more than they can handle now."

Hugh raised his hand. "May I ask —"

"No more questions please. I have too many things to do," she replied, flouncing out of the room.

Selecting four of the largest canvases, Hugh retired to a quiet corner of the terrace to paint. In short order he finished his task. But he didn't leave his works on the terrace. Carrying them down to the big stone gate beside a busy highway, he put them on display around the entrance to the estate. They were signs:

WELCOME TO THE CARNIVAL!
FREE RIDES! BRING THE KIDDIES!
FREE DRINKS FOR ALL!
PICNIC PARTIES WELCOME!

For some of his enterprises, Hugh worked, in 1937, in a loft off Fifth Avenue near Twenty-third Street. One of his projects was a mural design using a Rip Van Winkle theme for a Roger Smith hotel in the Catskills. He was also decorating large rolls of canvas, part of his mural for another Roger Smith hotel in Washington.

It entailed more work than he could handle but, by coincidence, he was approached just then by Bob Abbott, a young fellow also from Ithaca who was looking for a job. "As an adventuresome child of fourteen," said Bob, "I was determined to get the hell out of Ithaca and into a big city. Any big city would do. My brother gave me some letters to people he knew in New York, including Hugh Troy. I remembered Hugh only vaguely, mostly from hilarious stories about his escapades and his penchant for ridiculous, intricately planned hoaxes.

"Of all those to whom I gave the letters, Hugh was the only one who paid attention to me. He did so generously and immediately. We talked and he asked me to draw something. I forget what it was but he hired me at once as his paint boy. I remember vividly that he paid me weekly with a check for $125."

Bob didn't know what to do with the checks. He never needed money because Hugh always told him to keep the change every

". . . a mural design using a Rip Van Winkle theme . . ."

time he sent him on an errand. But one day Hugh confronted him.

"Say, Bob, what in hell are you doing with my checks?"

"Why, I've got 'em all in my wallet."

"In your wallet? No wonder they don't come back. Why didn't you take 'em to a bank?"

"Why, I didn't need the money. And I . . . I don't know much about banks."

"The next morning," recalls Bob, "Hugh took me to a bank to open a savings account."

"When Hugh found out I was living in a cramped little apartment at 103rd Street and West End Avenue, he was concerned enough about my welfare to pay me a surprise visit. That very day he yanked me out of that dump and got me into a basement apartment on Commerce Street just off Sheridan Square in the Village. The ceilings were so low there, though, that Hugh hated the place. He'd come in all bent over and, to avoid bumping his head, would crawl around crouched down like Groucho Marx. He'd often visit my grubby rooms after a night on the town and just stretch out on my couch or on the floor.

"We were really an odd pair. I was short and slight; he towered above me. In retrospect, I wonder why he liked me. It must have been that he just enjoyed having company. After asking for my opinion on something, he'd gravely listen to my answer as though it were worthy of consideration. He took me everywhere and treated me as an equal. Though I was naive, he insisted that I go along with him into many strange parts of the city, into atmospheres that otherwise I might never have experienced."

Bob had been working at his new job a few weeks when Hugh's Cornell classmate, Franchot Tone — he was then married to Joan Crawford — and Burgess Meredith, who was starring in a Broadway play, stopped in to see one of Hugh's murals. Dressed for the evening, they were on their way to catch someone's opening in the

Rainbow Room at the Waldorf Astoria.

"Say, Hugh," said Burgess, "why don't you come with us? Our cab's outside."

"All right. But only if Bob comes too."

"Okay, let's go."

"We can't go in these old rags covered with paint," said Hugh. "We'll have to change."

"We don't have time, Hugh, we're late now. You'll have to come that way."

"Oh, come on, Hugh," pleaded Franchot. We've got a lot of talking to do. I might not see you again for years."

Off they rushed to the Waldorf where their cab dropped them at the marquee. As they hurried toward the entrance, the doorman, a Colossus in blue uniform, brass buttons, and gold braid, spotted them. His mouth fell open. With two bounds, he planted his huge bulk in front of Hugh. "Where in hell do *you two* think you're going?" he growled, scowling at Hugh and Bob. "Beat it!"

"Hey, they're with us," protested Burgess.

"Sorry, sir. They can't come in."

"Oh, forget it, Burgess," said Hugh. "Bob and I'll just run along and —"

"*No!* Stay here, Hugh." said Burgess. He looked up at Colossus. "Where's Luigi, your maitre d'?"

"Oh, do you know Mr. Cassetta?"

"Sure. Get him out here."

Colossus punched a button. The maitre d' came running out.

"*Why, Mr. Meredith!* Come right in. I'm glad to —"

"Hold it, Luigi. We've got a problem. First, meet my friend, Franchot Tone, the actor. And this is —"

"*Mr. Tone!* I should have recog —"

". . . this is my good friend, the artist, Hugh Troy, and his assistant, Mr. Abbott. They didn't have time to dress. Can't you give us a table someplace where people won't notice us very much?"

"Well, Mr. Meredith . . . ah . . . I hate to say no . . . but I don't see how —"

Burgess pressed a bill into the hand of the maitre d' who flicked a glance at it.

"Well! . . . ah . . . let me think. There ought to be *some* way to — sure!" He turned to Colossus. "Say, George, would you skip down to our locker room and bring back three or four waiters' coats — different sizes? And a couple ties?"

Taking Hugh and Bob into the cloakroom, the maitre d' fitted them with the waiters' coats and ties.

"He led us all to a choice table," said Bob, "and seated us grandly right in the middle of all that splendor. I felt like Cinderella at the ball.

"I never thanked Hugh enough for that. He could have left me slaving away in the studio and I would have thought nothing of it. But, thanks to his generous insistence, I was taken along and, in the company of three celebrities, I reveled in the most enjoyable evening of my life."

That summer, Hugh's mother, whose health had not been good for years, began failing rapidly. She died in the fall of 1938. Elinor having left Ithaca after her graduation, Edith became the only companion of Professor Troy who was now retired.

Life for Professor Troy and Edith was now relieved by the frequent visits of Edith's boyfriend, "Doc" Alexander Zeissig, who was teaching in Cornell's Veterinary College. Edith, after marrying Doc the following year, persuaded the professor they could live happily together in the Oak Avenue house.

Fortunately, as this was perhaps the busiest time of Hugh's life, he found release from the sorrow of his mother's death in working on his many projects. He could express himself in two media: painting and writing. Besides a profile of Vincente Minelli, recently published in *Esquire,* he had also published two other articles, one in *Esquire,* the other in *The New Yorker,* both wry comments on amateur psychics. And he was painting murals for Washington's Ambassador Hotel. Then too, in preparation for the 1939 World's Fair, to be held near New York, he had secured mural commissions for the French and Swift pavilions.

The World's Fair canvases, he found, were too large for his studio. "So we embarked on a search for a new place," reminisces Bob Abbott, "and finally chose a former upholstering works in a loft on Third Avenue. It was over a French restaurant, the Chambord, good in its day but later to become famous.

"I was at that time enchanted with Edgar Allan Poe's works and, alone at night in that weird, gloomy loft, used to test its cavernous acoustics by a sonorous rendition of The Raven, which I loved. Once, oblivious to everything, I was squatted in the middle of a mural, reciting eloquently and ominously. I had reached the especially moving part:

> . . . and the silken, sad uncertain
> rustle of each purple curtain . . .

and was totally unaware that Hugh had arrived. Apparently he had walked quietly up the stairs. He let out a madman's howl, scaring the life out of me and making me feel like an absolute ass.

"Nearly every day he'd send me places: to Chinatown for sea horses, to Radio City Music Hall as his scout to report whether the current extravaganza was worth his catching later, or to lower East Side delis for corned beef goodies. Often, after arriving at a store, I'd get a clerk to help with my errand. Then, to my utter bewilderment, I'd be handed a telegram. I'd tear it open to find that Hugh had sent me a line from Edgar Allan Poe!

"Over a couple of months, he sent me, randomly, and a line or two at a time, almost all of *The Raven*. When I returned to the studio after receiving one of those messages, he'd only smile slightly and deadpan my mention of the wire. But, if I didn't bring it up, he'd ask, in a deep, sepulchral voice-of-doom-from-the-tomb, 'Did you get my message?' I'd respond with an imitation of his slight smile and deadpan nod. It seemed to suffice."

Eight

For a photographic record of his work, Hugh often worked with his fellow-Cornellian, the noted New York photographer Barrett Gallagher. Their friendship led to their working together on a spectacular project, the mural for Dario Toffenetti's restaurant on Times Square. Toffenetti's architect, Nat Owings, apparently figured Dario orbited in the same psychic plane as Hugh Troy. For Dario, asserting that "only a poet laureate could describe the taste of his food," composed his own menu notes "in prose so exuberant," said *The New Yorker*, "that they couldn't resist printing it." Take for example, Dario's description of his spaghetti: "one hundred yards of happiness."

"Dario, your dining room is going to have a blank wall fifteen feet high by sixty feet long," Owings told Toffenetti. "It would be ideal for a mural. And it just so happens that Hugh Troy is yearning to experiment with something new: a combination of oil on canvas and blown-up photographs."

"All right, Nat," Dario replied. "I want you to have Troy put there the most unusual mural ever painted." Hugh promised, with Gallagher's help, to turn out a job that would set Salvador Dali back on his heels.

While Gallagher went around the country photographing things, Hugh spread out canvas in his loft and painted. His photographs taken, Gallagher enlarged them to enormous size and, by elaborate geometry, fitted them to Hugh's portions. The painted parts, in pale greens and yellows, and the photographs, in sepia, matched perfectly.

The work being so complicated, on the day before the restaurant was billed to open, Hugh had covered only about three fourths of the wall space. Dario fretted. "Hugh," he chided, "it's going too slow. We open tomorrow morning."

"I know. Don't worry a bit, Dario," replied Hugh. "Just take it easy. It'll be ready. And say, when you go home tonight, would you please lock me in and leave some sandwiches and milk on the counter?"

"Sure, Hugh. Glad to do it."

Working all night, Hugh applied the finishing touches just as the first customers walked in for breakfast. As a result, Toffenetti's astonished patrons sat gaping at a wall as exciting as any electric sign on Broadway. Gay Nineties bicyclists, sea horses, milkmaids, starfish, and tree trunks blended fantastically into one another in a rhythmic writhing never seen before. Lewis Carrol would have loved it.

"The subject is *Madness*," Hugh explained to Toffenetti. "Masses mold into each other." Thus a bass viol turned into a bathing beauty, a race horse into a sea horse, a parasol into a Winged Victory, melons into talking machines. An ordinary cow stared moodily at the diners and the diners stared back, because the cow had the derriere of a fish. A lobster became inexorably in its hinder parts a Beau Brummell in silk hat and tails. Earlier, Hugh had girls on beaches turning into baked potatoes. But Toffenetti had said, "No sex!," so Hugh changed the girls into musical notes.

The mural delighted Toffenetti. In his peerless prose, he captioned it in words which wrapped up the theme very nicely: "A new melody comes to Broadway: "Ham and sweets, Idaho potatoes, and strawberry shortcake."

Happily, a good friend, watching Hugh's strenuous efforts on the mural, and sensing he needed a rest, invited him to spend a week-end at his country home in Bucks County, Pennsylvania. Seeing a chance to transfer a few pastoral scenes to canvas, Hugh brought his paints and brushes along.

The Post Office Department had just issued a new ruling that every RFD mailbox in the country had to display its owner's name. The sight of Hugh in his paint-spattered overalls (he was going to do a watercolor in the orchard) reminded his host of the new regulation. He asked if Hugh would mind lettering his mailbox for him.

"Sure," said Hugh. He ambled down to the lane entrance and was lettering away, chewing on a blade of grass, when a long, glossy car approached. With a shriek of protest from the tires, it shuddered to a stop. A pouter pigeon of a man slowly pulled a fat cigar from his mouth and called out, "Hey, bub! Yes, *you!* Whatcha charge for that job?"

The artist immediately became a yokel handyman. Pulling out the blade of grass, he poised it in midair.

"'Pends," he drawled. "Letters so big fetch six cent apiece. I also got a eight cent letter. Fancier. I call 'er 'Little Beaut.' "

The man flicked Hugh a visiting card. "Like to do my box this afternoon? Just up the road. Second house on the right."

"Plain letter or Little Beaut?"

The man grinned. "I'll take a chance on Little Beaut, bub."

"Okee-beebee-dokie," said Hugh. Then he added quickly, "Hold yer hosses a minute, boss." He studied the name on the card, pausing to scratch his head and stare at the sky while his lips and fingers did counting exercises. Finally he had it worked out.

"Comes to a dollar thutty-six," he said. "Call 'er a dollar thutty-

Hugh's mural in the former Toffenetti Restaurant, Times Square, New York

five even. Oke?"

"I think I can scrape up that much." And the long, glossy car moved down the road.

That afternoon Mr. Pouter was sitting on his terrace with his guests when a handsome new station wagon drew up at his mailbox below. A chauffeur, in whipcord and leggings, emerged and set up some beach chairs. Then a butler in a morning coat appeared, spread a luncheon cloth, and anchored it with an icebucket of champagne.

Now came a second station wagon, identical, bringing two incandescently beautiful girls wearing sunsuits, along with Hugh, still in his spattered overalls, still chewing grass.

The girls draped themselves in the chairs and accepted glasses of champagne. Hugh picked up a brush and a jar of paint. While the girls went "ooooh" and "aaaah" in admiration, he lettered the mailbox. Back on his terrace, the lord of the manor and his friends sat slack-jawed.

The job finished, the gangling handyman shambled up the terrace, performed an awkward bow, and said, "That'll be a dollar thutty-five, boss."

The landed proprietor handed it over. And now, the chauffeur and the butler packed up and the two station wagons departed, leaving the astonished people on the terrace to their own feverish conclusions.

Hugh couldn't resist a final touch. Two weeks later the owner of the artist's handiwork found, in his neatly lettered mailbox, a note on Hugh's letterhead. It said, "The Museum of Modern Art is preparing an exhibition of mailboxes I've done. Since I consider yours to be the finest example of my blue phase, would you be good enough to lend it?"

1940 saw Hugh bringing out the first of his three illustrated children's books, *Maud for A Day*. A mirthful tale which soon became a best seller, it earned an enthusiastic review in the New York Herald Tribune:

> Maud, official mascot mule of West Point, once had the colic on the eve of the Army and Navy game. What to do? Nothing but find the least mulish mule in the nearest mine shaft, bring her to the surface, pretty her up, and let her substitute for the occasion.
>
> So Marigold, who had more brains that you might think from her looks, found herself in the dead center of the game which has its wild moments and reaches the climax, Army 7, Navy 7. Time for just one more play.
>
> Just as the ball reached the sidelines, Marigold, the substitute for Maud, swung around and gave it the most famous kick in mule history, sixty yards over the Navy goalposts.
>
> In gratitude, they made her Brigadier Mascot, U.S.A., retired. She now lives on her retired pay in a beautiful green pasture in the Philadelphia suburb of Devon.

While working on his book, Hugh helped his friend, Put Brinley, finish Put's mural in the home office building of the Metropolitan Life Insurance Co. He then started a project for the Ithaca Yacht Club. Occupying nine panels on the walls of the club, the murals are tongue-in-cheek takeoffs on local history.

His visit to Ithaca also gave him a chance to see more of his friend, Patricia Carey, in whom he had been interested since childhood. Pat, a few years younger than Hugh — after graduating from Cornell, she had spent a year at the Sorbonne — was a good-looking, slender, auburn-haired girl. Hugh persuaded Pat, who was artistically inclined, along with Doc Zeissig and others, to help him with the Yacht Club murals. Of course, his trips to Ithaca now became more frequent.

"Marigold gave it the most famous kick in mule history,
sixty yards over the Navy goalposts."

Hugh managed to borrow a car for some of those trips and usually drove through the Holland Tunnel. At that time, 1941, to halt the spread of the Japanese beetle, many states inspected all cars crossing their borders. Returning to New York one day, Hugh pulled up at the Holland Tunnel pest control station.

"Carrying any plants or material harboring insects?" monotonously intoned the inspector for the thousandth time that day.

"Well, I do have three beetles with me," said Hugh, producing a

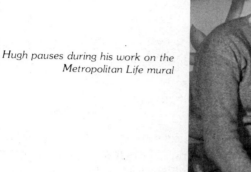
Hugh pauses during his work on the Metropolitan Life mural

small box.

"*Beetles?*" The inspector grabbed the box. After a boring day, he was eager for action. He peeked in the box. His eyebrows went up. He was staring, unknowingly, at three live cockroaches.

"Ah, ha! You understand, don't you, you can't take these into New York?"

"Oh, but they're my pet beetles. I'd hate to lose them. You mean if I don't take them into New York, I could keep them?"

"Well, I guess so."

"Say, look. I'll be coming back through here the day after tomorrow. Couldn't you just hold them here for me so I could pick them up on the way back?"

"We-e-e-ll, I don't know."

"*Please?*"

"Oh, all right. But it's quite irregular."

"Gee, thanks so much." Hugh handed him a small bottle.

"Here's their feed. Would you sprinkle a little of this powder in their box every morning?"

"We-e-e-ll, all right."

"Thanks an awful lot. Now, be careful. Don't give them too much. Just a small pinch will do. And I'll see you the day after tomorrow. Okay?"

"All right."

"Good-by. Thanks again."

Hugh's "beetles" are long gone as are the men who used to stand at the entrance to the tunnel collecting tickets that were sold in books to commuters. One collector greatly annoyed Hugh. To be sure of getting the ticket, the man would grasp, not only the ticket, but Hugh's fingers too. Hugh mulled over the problem. Soon he had a fitting solution.

Making a false hand of papier-mache', he used tape to stick the ticket to the fingers so it was visible. On his next trip he put the hand up his coat sleeve and held on to it as he approached the tunnel entrance.

The collector made his grab. Hugh sped away, leaving the horrified man holding the ticket and the hand, too.

For most New Yorkers, having a car has one disadvantage — no convenient place to park. But that didn't bother Hugh. He parked right at his front door next to a fire hydrant. (No one else would risk the huge fine for parking in such a spot.) He would then pick up the hydrant — a fake he had carved out of balsa wood — and hide it in the trunk of his car.

Whether conceiving such simple stunts or more elaborate hoaxes, Hugh's imagination was more than equal to the task. He especially delighted in a challenge such as that offered by his old classmate,

Harry Wade.

Harry was chairman of their fifteen-year reunion rally at Cornell. It was set for a Saturday in Bailey Hall auditorium with a few stage acts, a slide show, and the audience singing to organ music.

Harry thought of Hugh Troy and on Friday asked him for ideas. Hugh came up with a beauty and gave Harry the details. "Great," said Harry. "I'll get it all set up. You go out and get your props, Hugh."

With everything all set, Harry started the show.

"How about some singing?" said Harry. "We'll start with the Alma Mater. Organist, give us the key."

The organist hit his keys, trying to strike a chord. No music came out. Just a long *screeeech!* from his instrument.

"Hold it!" said Harry. "Is that the best you can do?"

The organist seemed embarrassed. He hit his keys again. *Screeeech!*

Harry snickered. "Sounds like a sick jackass. Our organ's got laryngitis," he anounced. "Anyone here know how to fix one of these things?"

Up the stairs to the stage, wearing overalls, trooped chief repairman Hugh Troy with many helpers. They carried ladders, hammers, pliers, big wrenches, enough tools to repair the Brooklyn Bridge. Hugh laid his ear against one of the organ pipes.

"Try it now," he commanded the organist.

"*Screeeech!*"

"Trouble's in this big one here," declared Hugh with authority, rapping the pipe. "Air's not getting through. We'll have to yank it down and see what's wrong."

With much wresting and wrenching, the men broke the straps that held the monster tube in place. After many grunts and groans, bangs and bumps, *crash!* — down came the pipe, a fake that Hugh had made to match the others, using gilded stovepipe.

"Why, no wonder," Hugh exclaimed. "*There's* part of your trouble." He reached into the pipe and pulled out, first, an old inner tube, then an old corset.

The audience laughed, then suddenly broke into a roar. Hugh had pulled out a live duck. It flew out of his hands, wheeled out over the crowd in two big circles, then landed on the arm of Hugh's classmate, Jack Syme.

Jack shook his arm but that made it mad. With a raucous *squaaawk!* it pulled its head back, then drove its beak into Jack's wrist.

"Ouch!", screamed Jack.

Meanwhile the house had broken out in pandemonium. Hugh had pulled out a second duck. It went into a barrel roll over the audience. Along its flight path, handkerchiefs were popping out. For, in an indiscreet way, the frightened fowl was celebrating its freedom by dropping whatever ducks drop.

Finally the commotion died down. Jack left to fix the wound in his wrist. Waiting in their room was his wife, Helen, who couldn't make the rally.

"Jack!", she cried. *"You're bloody.* What happened?"

"Honey, you're not going to believe this. I was bitten by a duck."

Hugh's success with his first children's book encouraged him to bring out another. In 1941 he finished his second, *The Chippendale Dam*. Critics praised it as a lighthearted bit of whimsy:

> Poor Widow Welch lived in a grand old house with her two pet beavers, Croton and Boulder. During a driving rainstorm, the leaky roof gives way. A flood of water cascading down the great staircase threatens to undermine the building.
>
> Croton and Boulder to the rescue! At last, a chance to prove themselves. They quickly build a dam of Widow Welch's Chippendale furniture, halt the flood, and save the house.
>
> The directors of the Metropolitan Museum discover and acclaim the unique Chippendale Dam and persuade the widow to sell it for eighteen bags of gold. You can

"Ducks in the Organ," as pictured by David Seavey

—David Seavey

"They quickly build a dam of Widow Welch's Chippendale furniture, halt the flood, and save the house."

now see it on display at the Metropolitan Museum of Art,
the world's one and only Chippendale Dam.

After Oxford University Press had published the book, their editor,
Dorrance, phoned Hugh one day.

"Hugh," he said, "a lady friend of mine in New Jersey thinks a
great deal of you."

"Really? Why is that?"

"Well, she's the head of a women's literary club over there and
they have just heard of your new book coming out. They'd be
thrilled if you would say a few words to them at one of their
meetings. So I told them I would get you to talk to their group."

Dorrance had involved Hugh in too many affairs like that. Hugh
found them utterly boring but did not want to turn Dorrance down
directly. Then an idea clicked through Hugh's brain.

"Well, Dorrance, I wouldn't have to go to New Jersey, would I?"

"Oh, that's where they always meet."

"Couldn't they come to my studio? It's in a loft on Third Avenue."

"Do you really mean it? Why, I'm sure they'd *love* it."

"All right. Tell your friend to call me. We'll work out a date."

To prepare for his lecture, Hugh dispatched Bob Abbott on a series
of errands . . . down the block to an undertaker for twenty wooden
folding chairs, each labeled on the back in big, black letters:

MELTZER MORTUARY

. . . to a restaurant supply house for a couple of dozen yellow
crockery bowls with green rings . . . to a second-hand store for a
bunch of oversized soup spoons . . . to Shelton's Delicatessen for
an outrageous selection of cold cuts, salads, sauerkraut, and garlic
pickles.

Came the great day. Up in the creaky old elevator to the Troy
studio came the bevy of biddies. Bowing deeply in a grand manner,
Hugh ushered them in. Costumed in what he hoped was their idea

of what a great artist might wear, he was an image from Toulouse-Lautrec's Left Bank era in a big, floppy beret and long, flowing smock and with a ten-inch cigarette holder cocked toward the ceiling.

Leading them into his study, the maestro ensconced them in the mortuary chairs. They were close to a large mural on the floor over which Bob hovered, making believe he was working.

The head biddy rose. She recounted the achievements of Hugh Troy and told her friends how fortunate they were that he would invite them to his sanctum. She introduced the great man and sat down.

Hugh stood up. Expressing his delight at being honored by their presence, he launched his lecture. He spoke clearly at first. But after a while it became harder to understand him. Now and then he would lapse into double-talk. (He had gone so far in preparing for his lecture that he had paid for and taken lessons in double-talk from a Broadway comic.)

Finally his speech became all double-talk. The smiles on the ladies' faces slowly faded away. Their brows started to wrinkle. They leaned forward, striving to hear more clearly.

Hugh had arranged for Bob, wearing his smock and slippers, and apparently engrossed in his work, to slither on his knees around the edges of the mural some thirty feet away from the group. Now and then, as Hugh had coached him, Bob would crank a squeaky old upholstering gadget he was carrying.

Hearing the squeak from the gadget, Hugh would stop talking, whirl around, and yell at Bob, *"Stop plunking the oleanbix!"* Then he'd quietly face the ladies as though nothing had happened and resume his double-talk. A few minutes later, to their bewilderment, he'd hear the squeak and scream at Bob again. (He had told Bob ahead of time to let things settle down a bit after each incident then make more noise with his gadget.)

Finally he concluded: "My dear ladies, you have been a most delightful audience. We could go on discussing the future of art but I know you must leave soon. Won't you please come to my apartment for refreshments?"

The flabbergasted females trooped back into the decrepit elevator and down to Third Avenue. With the artist as their guide, they played follow-the-leader down the sidewalk to his apartment.

Here he proudly showed them his spread from Shelton's. Seated on more mortuary chairs, they nibbled potato chips, head cheese, and limburger. From paper cups they swilled beer, soda water, and orange crush. After a while, Hugh disappeared.

He returned attired in pajamas cut from flannel bearing kiddie designs: Little Jack Horner, The Cow Jumped Over the Moon, and Little Miss Muffet. On his feet: bunny slippers with beady glass eyes. In his arms he carried the crockery bowls while his hands clutched the big spoons.

"Here you are," he said, "one for you, one for you, and one for *you*." With a disarming smile, he handed a bowl and spoon to each of his guests who were still valiantly striving to enjoy everything despite their confusion. One of them asked, "What are these bowls for?"

"Ah! Surprise! A special dessert," Hugh said. Beckoning them to follow, he led them to his bathroom. With a wave of his hand, he directed their gaze to his bathtub.

In it, shimmering in the glare from the fly-specked bare bulb dangling from the ceiling, quivered a pool of lemon Jell-O. Congealed in the gelatinous block were little favors: penny candy, licorice hats, Chinese sea horses, and gum balls. Their host stood there, proudly holding a big ladle, ready to fill their bowls.

Gingerly, a few of the more daring proffered their dishes. Hugh gave each a gob of the goo. They left, sat in their chairs, then poked half-heartedly at the delicacy. No one asked for seconds.

The poor dears barely survived. Bowing deeply as they left, Hugh accepted their thanks with profound humility, stressing again how overwhelmed he was with the honor of their visit.

Dorrance was enraged. Never again did he commit Troy to talk to any of his literary groups.

Nine

When the Japanese attacked Pearl Harbor on December 7, 1941, among the millions of Americans affected were Hugh and his brother, Fran, who, in 1942, received their draft notices. It also brought Hugh's courtship of his girl, Pat, to a head. They were married in Ithaca in a simple ceremony.

The newlyweds' time together after the wedding was all too short. Soon afterward, Hugh was off to Connecticut for his induction into the Air Corps. Wouldn't you suppose that Hugh, with a background of dubious military value, would be tucked away in some obscure cubbyhole as a lowly buck private? Well, guess again. Here's Hugh:

I was inducted in a huge building near Hartford, Connecticut, and I recall those long lines, as far as you could see, of naked men, each clutching a brown paper bag that held an apple and a cheese sandwich. The food was to eat if we got hungry while going through the different booths. It was fascinating. I'd never been through anything like that before.

I finally entered a room with about eight desks. It was late in the afternoon so most of the men normally at the desks had gone home. At the last desk sat a man with three huge volumes that listed all the MOS (Military Operation Specialty) numbers in the service.

He also had a machine for punching IBM cards. He'd

put your card in his machine, hit some buttons, and the machine would punch your card with your MOS number. Once he punched your card with that number, you were *stuck* with it, *for life*. That was the number that determined the course of your training and, thus, your whole career in the service.

"Which do you like best," he asked me, "to write or to paint?"

"Why, neither," I said. "I like 'em both."

"Well you have to tell me one so I can give you a number."

"I do 'em both well," I said, "and I don't want any of your numbers."

"Well," he said, "I've gotta give you *some* number."

He stuck my card in his machine and was going to punch it for me. But just then the phone rang at one of the vacant desks and he left to answer it. While his back was turned, I reached over to his machine and quickly gave my card eight wild punches. As a result, according to my card, I was qualified as, of all things, a *demolition expert!*

Now, I've always been deathly afraid of handling anything like dynamite or TNT. But now they wanted me to *teach it!* And — would you believe it? — I wound up as a second lieutenant in the Air Force Intelligence School and was put on the staff! And those eight wild punches did it all.

After receiving instructions in handling explosives, Hugh overcame his aversion to them and established a training school at an Air Force base on Long Island. There, after rigging a house with booby traps, he would show a group of recruits how to find and defuse them. Later, as a demolitions expert, he toured the country to teach personnel at other bases.

Lieutenant Troy

During the second phase of his training in 1943, Hugh, then Lieutenant Troy in B Company of an engineer outfit, was stationed at the Army Air Base, (Byrd Field) Richmond, Virginia. Stuck behind a desk, he was loaded down with reports, reports, and more reports. He had to account for the most trivial details of camp operation and his reports, bales and bundles of them, went in to the Pentagon.

He soon became browned off at the avalanche of paperwork that fell on his desk every day. A good half of it was utterly futile, he told his C.O.; he was learning nothing and getting nowhere, and his contribution to the war effort was a big, fat, empty zero.

His C.O. lived by The Book. "If Washington wants you to do this paperwork," he said, "you'll do it. Yours not to reason why. Surely you're not suggesting that a mere lieutenant knows more than the

Chief of Staff of the Army of the United States?"

The operative word was "mere." It cocked a trigger which a gnat's weight — or a fly's, as it happened — could trip.

One August afternoon Lieutenant Troy was inspecting one of the messhalls. Though the summer was well along, window screens had not been issued. So the mess sergeants, to keep the flies down, had hung up half a dozen of those sticky flypaper spirals. Troy saw them and the trigger tripped.

Back in his office, he conceived and drew up a form:

FLYPAPER REPORT

B Company Messhall. Date: _____

Flypaper No. 1:
   Flies this week: _____
   Flies last week: _____
   Gain/loss (strike out one):   _____
Flypaper No. 2:
   Flies this week: _____
   (and so on)

And so went the report for all six flypaper spirals. Then he ran off a sheaf of copies, filled in random figures on the top one, worked out the averages and the grand totals, and sent the form along with the weekly bundle going to the Pentagon, keeping a carbon for his files. His plan was to let the weekly carbons pile up for a month, then spread them in front of the C.O.: "See, sir, I told you nobody reads our gibberish!"

The month ended without an echo, and Hugh was gathering his carbons for the confrontation when a distraught lieutenant burst into the office. "*You Troy?*" Thank God I caught you! I'm from A Company. Listen, what's all this about some Flypaper Report I'm supposed to turn in? The Old Man just got a rocket from Washington, asking why his Flypaper Reports weren't complete, and he's chewing out every adjutant on the base. I wouldn't know a Flypaper Report if it pinned a medal on me, but my clerk says he heard your clerk mention 'em. Brief me, will you?"

Troy reeled. With a feeling that he had sown the wind and someone was about to reap the whirlwind, he brought out one of his forms and explained how to complete it.

"Gotcha!" the lieutenant said. "Thanks! — but *wait,* hold on a minute! There's one thing here I don't get. You say 'flies this week' and 'flies last week.' When you check your flypapers, how do you tell last week's flies from this week's?"

A genius capable of the grand conception of the Flypaper Report was also capable of working out its details. "A very good question," Troy assured him. "You're the first one who has had the vision to ask it. The answer is," — and it came to him at that instant — "I have a sergeant follow me around with a matchstick and a saucer of ketchup, and as I count each fly, he daubs it. Simple! No sweat at all. Some sergeants prefer mustard as a dauber, but we here in B Company find that ketchup has a certain something that mustard lacks."

The lieutenant glowed. "Well, I've got the pitch now. Thanks a million, chum! If it hadn't been for you, my wife would be addressing my letters, 'P.F.C.' "

He rushed out, almost colliding with a C Company officer, entering with one from D Company. It developed that they had to turn in some flypaper reports — or else; and what in the name of Robert E. Napoleon was a "flypaper report"? Troy sighed and reached into his drawer for some more forms . . . .

From that day on, every bundle of reports that went to Washington included page after page of Flypaper Reports and, for all Hugh knows, the Pentagon made them standard procedure for all the armed forces.

Detached from the engineers some time later, Hugh never

"The Flypaper Reports," as pictured by Tom Wolfe

learned whether his whirlwind harmlessly blew itself out, or cut a swath of devastation. But as he left, he suspected that somewhere in the Pentagon there was a Flypaper Report Section, and that its C.O., a full colonel, spent half his time writing petitions in triplicate for "personnel increments" so that he'd be able to discharge his duties with the thoroughness their importance deserved.

Even while in training, Hugh found time to finish writing his third children's book, Five Golden Wrens, by far his best. Indeed, it won a New York Herald Tribune prize as the best children's book of 1943 and a glowing review:

> When The Chippendale Dam burst into children's literature, we recognized not only originality but a gift for getting into the spirit of a period and writing of it in its own idiom. Both traits show ever more clearly in Lieutenant Troy's new, best book, the story of a king who wore a crown with a radio attachment and found that it made his royal head more than usually uneasy. Written in the vein of the fairy-tale age, the contrast between this and the up-to-date nature of the story is refreshingly piquant.
>
> The king's mind was so upset by news broadcasts that he was on the verge of acute melancholia when five golden wrens, magic, no doubt, mistook his crown for a birdhouse, settled in it, and set up so sweet a song that the king thought he had tuned in on a secret radio station. He wakes in the morning and says, "How much better to start the day with this wonderful broadcast than to be awakened by a recital of all the bad things that happened in the night."
>
> His nerves settled, the kingdom prospered, the scullery maid whom the wrens had deserted made the best of it, and a rival queen laid a dark plot to get the

wrens away for a wren pie.

Following the failure of the wicked queen's plot, king and scullery maid are brought together. They marry. Children are expected. Happiness is restored to the kingdom.

How everything came out well is told with the aid of many of Lieutenant Troy's pictures, bold, clear designs as funny as the story. It's a gay, ingenious fantasy.

Like those other great children's classics, A. A. Milne's Pooh stories, Hugh's tales are rare combinations of serene inocence and ironic sophistication that can be read with perennial delight by either child or adult. They clearly are also comments on humanity and the world.

Hugh's books were successful for one reason above all: his remarkable rapport with children. Pat commented on this after Hugh died. "There was a lot of the child in Hugh. And he never lost it. For instance, he invented many stories for his niece during his visits to her home. One series told of the fantastic adventures of Shirley Temple, then at the peak of her popularity.

"Having extended the tales over many visits, Hugh got awfully tired of Shirley Temple, even though the situations he kept getting her into were quite unlike those of her movies. He ended the series very dramatically. She was run over by a steam roller and flattened out like a paper doll. The little girl loved the ending. Hugh had made it as improbable and fanciful as all the rest. He could reach children. They shared the same vision."

By 1944, Hugh, now a first lieutenant, had moved with Pat to Florida where he was stationed near Orlando teaching target recognition at the Army Air Corps Tactical Air Center. He also taught similar classes for the Navy. Eventually, he was assigned to the

After the King and the maid were married, the Wrens flew back and forth all day between the radio-crown and their Queen's hat. The King ordered a microphone so that their golden melody was shared by all his subjects.

South Seas. He wound up on Saipan with General Curtis LeMay's 21st Bomber Command, 20th Air Force, as an air reconnaissance officer. But his duties involved more than air reconnaissance. In Hugh's words:

> I was with an advance party, just a few B-29's, on Saipan in the Marianas group where the island people were Chamorros. Most of them were loyal but we were a little leery of them, so we kept them locked up in compounds. Only the children were allowed outside.
>
> We'd just got settled in there when this good-looking, tall, bearded man wearing U. S. insignia showed up. He was a civilian folklorist named Atherton from the Library of Congress whose job was to collect the legends of the Marianas.
>
> He shouldn't have been there. His superiors must have been confused, however, and figured the islands

General Curtis LeMay.

were secure. But they weren't. So my boss, General Nichol, called me in.

"Captain Troy," he said, "we can't have this fellow here. Will you see that he gets whatever he wants? Then get him to hell off this damned island before he gets killed."

"Yes, sir," I replied. "I'll take care of him."

I talked to the folklorist and, lo and behold, learned that he had brought along seven quarts of whiskey. That was a smart idea on his part because whiskey was practically a medium of exchange. You could swap a quart or two for almost anything. I was interested because, being an advance party, we were on short rations. We hadn't seen liquor for weeks.

Every morning I had to drive to a little bombed-out town on the coast to bring in our mail. And on those trips I'd often take along a little Chamorro boy named Emmanuel who was allowed to leave the compound. He was a sweet little kid who spoke English, having gone to an American school. His parents having been killed in the war, he was living with his grandfather.

After I talked to the folklorist, I picked up Emmanuel as usual the next morning. I could see the makings of a deal.

"Look, Emmanuel," I said, "if I were to tell you some stories in English, could you tell the same stories in Chamorro?"

"Sure," said Emmanuel.

"Fine," I said. "Now, if I bring a visitor, a very nice gentleman, to your grandfather's hut, would you tell *him* the stories in Chamorro?"

"Sure," said Emmanuel, "but why?"

"Well," I said, "he likes to collect stories. Now here's what I'll do. For every story you tell the gentleman, I'll give you three comic books and three Hershey bars. But you mustn't tell anyone else about it. And you must be sure to tell the gentleman that your grandmother used to tell you the stories before you went to bed at night. Okay?"

"Sure, fine," said Emmanuel.

So that took care of Emmanuel's part in my scheme. Then I wangled a deal with the folklorist. "Atherton," I said, "suppose I were to get a true local legend for you. Would it be worth a quart of whiskey?"

"Of course," he said. "But how can *you* get any legends?"

"Why, I have a friend," I said, "a little Chamorro boy who knows them. But he tells them in Chamorro of course."

"No problem," said Atherton. "I'll just bring my interpreter along."

"Okay," I said. "I'll set it up and let you know."

Every night after that my buddies and I would have a long bull session in our tent. We called our confab "The Children's Hour" and in it we wrote the legends of old Saipan. I cooked up a literary goulash using a portion of Aesop's Fables, a goodly gob of Mother Goose, and a dash of Winnie the Pooh.

Each time I picked up Emmanuel I'd teach him the story we'd dreamed up the night before. Then I'd go and get Atherton.

"Hop in, Atherton," I'd say. "We're going over to the compound."

He'd grab his interpreter and we'd all go over to the hut of Emmanuel's grandfather. The old man would sit on the floor smoking his pipe while the young fellow rattled off this tall tale I'd taught him. The interpreter would take it all down in shorthand while Atherton sat there beaming, simply thrilled at the way things were going. A couple of days later we'd do another story. This went on until I had all of Atherton's whiskey. He finally flew back to Washington with his marvelous collection of legends.

But one thing puzzled me. Everytime we went through that rigmarole and Emmanuel had finished talking, his grandfather would spout a line of gibberish to him, all in Chamorro of course. So, after I'd got all the whiskey and Emmanuel was loaded up with comic books and Hershey bars, I askd the boy about it.

"Tell me something," I said. "What was it your grandfather said every time you finished telling one of those stories?"

"Oh," said Emmanuel, "he'd say, 'where in the world did you *ever* hear such a lot of horse manure?' "

Ten

By 1945, the fourth year of our long, tough war, our Air Corps, Navy, and GI's had pushed the Japs back from island to island in the Pacific. With our planes in full command of the air, no Japanese vessel was safe.

Every time we bombed Jap ships, in order to assess the damage, our flyboys followed up and shot pictures. General LeMay's team of photo interpreters then examined them and reported their findings. When one of the men on this team left, a colonel assigned Hugh to replace him because Hugh was an expert in that line.

Since Hugh's training had all been on land, interpreting naval photos had a few quirks that Hugh didn't appreciate, especially the use of nautical terms. Boat people have always been testy about sticking to naval terminology — fore and aft instead of front and rear; port and starboard for left and right; you walk on decks and not on floors; you sleep in bunks, not beds; food is prepared in a galley, not a kitchen; and a toilet, of course, is always called a head.

Copies of Hugh's reports of bombing results always went to the Navy. When the Navy got them, they would always nitpick the language. After being dressed down a few times, Hugh became teed off at their insistence on using the correct nautical terms. So, tongue in cheek, after a large Japanese ship was bombed, he produced this report:

> Photos show this big Jap boat is hurt real bad. Its floors
> are all torn up, front, center, and rear. The chimney has
> been knocked down as well as its two flagpoles. Many
> lifeboats are unusable, their hangers being torn apart.
> There is a big hole in its left side, but the boat is leaning to
> the right, showing that a torpedo may have pierced the
> cellar wall on that side. Hole in center floor shows kit-
> chen stoves strewn about on floor below. Some dam-
> aged beds can be seen. Attack took place about 3 PM so
> we would estimate boat would turn over about seven
> bells.

Twelve hours after the Navy got the message, Hugh was ordered to
report to General LeMay on the double and bring his file of reports.
Grabbing his file, he legged it to LeMay's headquarters.

LeMay, big, beefy, bushy-browed, a bull in a man's body, with a
cigar grafted onto the side of his mouth, glared at Hugh. After
chomping on the cigar, he pulled it out, spat a speck off his tongue,
then barked, "Dammit, Captain Troy, you've got me in trouble."

"Trouble, sir?"

"Your report on that damned Jap ship. Got your file there?"

"Yes, sir."

"Gimme your last report."

Hugh held it out. LeMay snatched it, jammed his cigar back in his
mouth, and read it.

"Hmmm. Well, Captain Troy, you . . . ah . . . you've got plenty of
facts there. But I'll tell you something. The Navy doesn't like it one
damned bit. And, the way they talked, I've gotta *do something*
about you. Well . . . ah . . . listen. Consider yourself reprimanded.
Understand?"

"Yes, sir."

"That's all. You may go."

Hugh saluted. He was halfway to the door when LeMay barked again. "Captain Troy!"

"Yes, sir."

"If you get a chance, do it to the bastards again."

During the war years, Valerie, the young daughter of Hugh's close friend and fellow-Cornellian, Walt Nield, kept up a running correspondence with her "Uncle Hugh." Her memories of him are those of a child who saw him as "a very vulnerable, warm, and endearing man who responded to children with a childlike quality of his own." Valerie was surprised to learn what Hugh had done with her February, 1945 valentine.

> Dear Valerie,
>   I have my beautiful valentine from you pinned up on a coconut tree near my tent so all the military personnel may gaze on it with envy.
>   They all want to know who the very talented "Val" is and if she is my own true love.
>   Of course, I say,. "Yes, she is the light of my life."
>
> Many thanks and love,
Uncle Hugh

And she was intrigued when Hugh described the strange animals on Saipan. One of his letters bore a sketch of a mammoth "lizard that guards our tent at night." Another portrayed one of Saipan's feathered, bespectacled creatures that "are very kind and provide us with fresh eggs. They are only two inches high, so the eggs are small."

Hugh left for Guam after we had captured that island and built an

". . . a lizard guards our tent at night."

airport. There, as a story teller *par excellence,* he became the center of a group of friends with time on their hands, former newspapermen who were handling the public relations of the 20th Air Force. In their long confabs, Hugh's yen for imaginative exercises stimulated them to produce a legendary figure, Senora Cuevas, the widow of the first governor of Guam. As Hugh vividly described her later:

"Senora Cuevas was a member of Cornell's class of 1895, my father's class, and had founded the Cornell Women's Mandolin and Glee Club. On Guam, she lived in a three-story Victorian house

". . . they provide us with fresh eggs. They are only two inches high so the eggs are small."

built between the runways of the airfield, an exact replica of her old family home in Hoboken, complete even to the cast iron deer on the lawn.

"When assassins killed her husband, she refused to go back to the States but remained in her home, doing good works for the Guamanians and carrying on the work of her husband. She had even donated her furniture to Guam's social club, the Royal Palms Hallowe'en and Foxtrot Society, and had organized a school to prepare young native boys for Andover and Yale.

"Naturally she became so beloved by the natives that when the Japs came, they left her completely alone for they knew that any harm to her would start mass uprisings. The Commanding General of the Jap forces, however, did deign to call on her soon after they landed. After accepting a cup of tea and some sweet cakes, he suddenly died from an attack of acute indigestion.

"After we had retaken Guam, our Seabees had to build an airstrip long enough to handle our B-29's. The senora owned the only available land so the Seabees wanted to demolish her mansion. But they finally settled for a runway on each side of her house. She became the guardian of all the air crews on the field and, although her boys' planes often knocked the chanticleer off her weathervane, she was never angry so long as her engineer friends replaced it each time.

"The amazing lady even had our Signal Corps install a miniature control board near the altar of her Spanish-style chapel. That way, she could keep track of her boys on every flight and pray for their safe return.

"One thing above all endeared her to the enlisted men — the big parties she threw every Saturday night. Her cellar was well stocked and she was generous with it. At these affairs, she'd tolerate generals and colonels but only on condition that they pass the drinks for the enlisted men."

After Hugh had returned to the States and had nearly forgotten about Senora Cuevas, he happened to pick up a copy of the *Reader's Digest*. Its feature item, titled "The Most Unforgettable Character I Ever Met," caught his eye. Forthwith he unlimbered his typewriter, wrote up Senora Cuevas's story in detail, and sent it off to the magazine with a note asking whether they might be interested.

In just a few days he had a phone call.

"Mr. Troy, this is Ben Loomis. I'm an editor at *Reader's Digest* and wanted you to know we liked your article. In fact, it's just the kind of story we're looking for."

"Well, I'm glad to hear that, Mr. Loomis."

"Yes, we're willing to pay liberally for it. But may I suggest something that would make it more valuable?"

"Sure, what's that?"

"Pictures. Surely you have photographs somewhere, of the island, or the airport or, better yet, that mansion. Or even Senora Cuevas?"

"Oh! Well . . . ah . . . you know, in all the packing and unpacking so much of my stuff was lost. I feel terrible about it. Tell you what I do have though, a sketch of the house that's almost as good as a photo. It shows Senora Cuevas on the front porch."

"Really? That might fill the bill. Why don't you mail it to me?"

"I'll do better. I'll bring it in myself. Okay?"

"Fine. We'll be expecting you."

Working into the morning hours, Hugh produced his sketch. It showed the island with its mountains and, in front of them, the rococo residence of the senora, situated between the two runways and surrounded by an iron picket fence. On the spacious lawn you can see the cast iron deer and the little white chapel. And on the porch of the edifice stands the illustrious lady herself in a long, black gown, waving to her boys in the B-29's flying overhead.

Off to the *Digest* offices went Hugh, the sketch under his arm.

"Why, Mr. Troy," said Loomis, "this isn't a *sketch*. It's a finely

The Cuevas mansion. "Working into the morning hours, Hugh produced his sketch."

detailed drawing, a work of art! It will print *perfectly*. Now, as to payment. Would say, five hundred be satisfactory?"

"You're very generous."

"Not at all," said Loomis. With those words, he walked Hugh down the hall toward the door.

As fate would have it, along the corridor came another editor on the magazine, an old friend of Hugh's.

"Why, *Hugh Troy!* What in hell are *you* doing here?"

Out came the story. After Hugh had left, the second editor suggested that Loomis carefully check the tale of Senora Cuevas. He did.

A few days later Hugh received a letter from the *Digest*.

"With much regret," it said, "We are returning your sketch and your manuscript of your apparently fictional character. Our check went out yesterday. When it arrives would you please return it?"

Hugh had nearly gotten away with it. It was his greatest unperpetrated hoax.

During Hugh's years away, Pat found many ways to keep busy. For a while she was the personal secretary for Anne Lindbergh. Later, through her interest in art, she became acquainted with Mrs. Vanderbilt Webb, a philanthropist who had founded America House. It was an arts and crafts shop and studio on New York's East Forty-third Street.

When he returned from the war, Hugh found Pat engrossed in her work at America House and desirous of keeping at it for a while. That was just a detail, though, compared to their biggest problem, finding a place to live. So many servicemen were returning to New York that locating an apartment seemed impossible. But Mrs. Webb, coming to their rescue, found a place for them not far from where she lived, Garrison, N.Y.

Garrison is a small settlement on the hilly east bank of the Hudson, forty miles north of Manhattan. Here, for decades, the most exciting daily event was either the arrival of a New York Central train or the docking of the Hudson River ferry. In a note to an Ithaca friend he affectionately called "Aunt Madge," Hugh described his new home:

> Dear Aunt Madge
>
> We're living in an abandoned eagle's nest on a mountain top. The clouds float in one window and out the other and sometimes there are minor thunderstorms in the broom closet.
>
> Come and see. It's wonderful. Pat joins me in love to you all.
>
> Hugh

From their rustic, ranch-style home in a large grove on "The Ridge," Pat and Hugh had a clear, restful view of the broad Hudson and its river traffic. Here, in a bucolic setting, Hugh settled down to a relaxing country life, combining work with long rambles over Garrison's many hills. While writing a new children's book, he painted an occasional mural. Through a friend, John Escher, a publisher of juvenile periodicals, he arranged to draw four comic strips weekly for *Young America* and *The Weekly Reader*.

Hugh wasn't the only person leaving the service to settle in Garrison. Among his neighbors were Gene Rayburn, familiar to TV viewers, and his wife, Helen. The Troys and Rayburns found they had not only common problems but common interests.

"What a dear, sweet woman Pat was," recalls Helen. "And how we loved Hugh, a gentle funny man. After we became acquainted, he gave our little girl a copy of *The Chippendale Dam* and inscribed a beautiful drawing on its flyleaf for her. He was so kind and loving and, above all, so entertaining, that we always loved to hear him talk."

Hugh's home on "The Ridge" in Garrison, N.Y. "We're living in an abandoned eagle's nest on a mountain top."

Hugh's mural in the former Ivy Room of Cornell's Willard Straight Hall.

In Ithaca for a lengthy visit during the Christmas season, Hugh spent most of his time painting a mural in the Ivy Room of Cornell's Willard Straight Hall. It showed the goddess Minerva, surrounded by a score of studious owls, returning from the world's battlefields to the Ivy League seats of learning.

Royal "Red" Woodin, who was then studying architecture, was flattered when Hugh asked him to help with the project. As they were painting away, each of them up on a ladder, and the floor littered with their tarpaulins, brushes, paints, and thinners, Lewis, the manager, showed up.

"You fellows gotta clear the floor when you're through tonight."

"*Tonight!*" said Hugh. "We've got another day's work ahead of us."

"Doesn't matter. You've gotta clear the floor. I'm bringing in the night crew to wax and polish it."

"Good Lord! Where'll we put all this stuff?"

"I don't care where you put it," said Lewis as he left the room.

"Here, Red," said Hugh, handing him a five dollar bill, "run down to the hardware store and get about three dozen big screw hooks and a few dozen feet of heavy wire."

"What for?" said Red.

"Oh, I'll show you later on."

"I brought the stuff back," said Red, "and toward the end of the day Hugh called me over. 'Lewis told us he didn't care where we put our stuff,' said Hugh. 'So let's screw all these hooks into the ceiling.' After we screwed in all the hooks, we hung all our tarps up there. Then we used the wire to hang up our brushes and all our cans and bottles of paint and thinner. Finally we hung up our ladders, inverted, just as though we had been working upside down.

" 'Gee,' said Hugh, 'I'd give a lot to see the faces of Lewis and his crew when they show up.' "

Back in his home in Garrison, Hugh, in his spare time, worked on solving a problem that had bothered him ever since he and Pat had moved in. Although their home was spacious, modern and afforded a spectacular view, it had one small drawback. It was directly across the river from the West Point Military Academy. So, at an unseemly hour every morning the clear, piercing notes of the Academy bugles would disturb their sleep.

Pat was reconciled to it. She looked on it simply as a disadvantage of living in that spot, something they would have to endure. She didn't know Hugh had a plan for abating the nuisance until she heard him talking to a clerk in a New York music store.

"Got any records of bugle calls?"

"Bugle calls? I'm afraid we don't have a thing like that in stock.

But we could order it for you."

"Will it have 'reveille' on it?"

"Reveille? Must you have that?"

"Yes. You see, we live right across the river from West Point and their damned bugles wake us up every morning at six o'clock. I've got an amplifier and loudspeaker. And, as soon as I get that record, I'm going to blast them out of their bunks at five A.M."

"I pulled it off one morning," Hugh told a friend later, "and watched the effect through my binoculars. A line of men came streaming out of a building rubbing their eyes, but an officer herded them back in and pointed across the river.

"They got my message, all right. After that they toned their darned bugles down."

By the fall of 1948, after completing twenty-two poems for juveniles, Hugh described them in a letter to his friend, Laura Bryant, the music director of Ithaca's public schools:

Dear Aunt Laura,

Greetings, and here is something that you may be able to help me out on. I have just about finished a new book of verse for children which will be published next year. I have included verses for the feast days, and particularly, the enclosed one for Christmas.

I am hoping that with this one, I can persuade the publisher to also print the music for this verse, as I have written it with the idea in mind that it should be sung.

I've always loved the carol, "The First Day of Christmas," and of course that can't be beat. But I have in mind something a bit haunting, and maybe even the verse would lend itself to a response treatment with Santa singing his lines and the lighter voices carrying the questions. You will also note the word "No" at the beginning of each last line of the choruses. This word is outside the rhyme scheme and could probably be used effectively as a sort of hold or perhaps almost a shout if sung by children who drink their blackberry cordial straight.

SEVEN SECRETS

> I fell asleep dreaming of Christmas
> And when I awoke, I'd have sworn
> I found old Santa Claus snoozing
> In front of our fire Christmas morn.
>
> I wakened him gently by tweaking
> The tip of his Kriss Kringle nose.
> Before he dashed off, Santa told me
> These secrets I shouldn't disclose:
>
> Oh, what did you bring for dear mother?
> "A lark," Santa whispered to me.
> A lark we can have with each other?
> "No? A lark singing sweet in a tree."

In any event, it should be very simple and sort of in the manner of an old French or English folk song. Maybe there's a tune already floating around in your wonderful bean that might work out.

I imagine we won't be up that way until Christmas time, when we hope to see you. Pat sends best and joins me in fond memories of Coffee Cake a la Laura.

Anxiously,
Hugh

Though his book was nearly completed, it was not to be published. Events in Europe brought all Hugh's plans — for finishing the book and for illustrating the children's magazines — to an abrupt end.

Eleven

By 1950, after its blockade of Berlin, Russia had stepped up the cold war. Our government then began to expand its clandestine action arm, the Central Intelligence Agency. From less than five thousand employees in 1950, the CIA was to grow to fifteen thousand by 1955.

One of Hugh's friends of his New York days, Joe Bryan, III, an author and Navy veteran, was responsible for part of that growth. Bryan, a former managing editor of *Town and Country* and associate editor of the *Saturday Evening Post,* was hired to organize a Political and Psychological Warfare Section. When he began staffing the section in 1950, he remembered Hugh's talents as a writer and artist and offered him a job.

No doubt the offer flattered and surprised Hugh. Still, it was opportune. In the post-war inflation, prices were rising. His income from murals was negligible, and that from his writing barely met his expenses. The assurance of a liberal salary and the opportunity to exercise his talents in service to his country at a time of need were appealing. Author Howard Hunt, Hugh's co-worker, notes the outcome in his book, *Undercover:* "Artist-illustrator Hugh Troy joined Bryan's staff and formed a highly competent group of political cartoonists and polemicists." For Hugh, it meant, of course, a move to Washington.

After he had rented a home on N Street, he came back to the office with a feeling of satisfaction. He told Joe Bryan all about it. Bryan wasn't above a little leg-pulling himself. "Oh, Hugh!" he exclaimed. "Not *that* house?"

"Why?" replied Hugh. "What's wrong with it?"

"Well, you should have checked on your neighbors. Did you find out who lives next to you?"

"No."

"Why, it's that dreadful Mrs. Blatherstein. And do you know who lives across the street?"

"No."

"You don't? That's Mrs. Snidely. Boy, is *she* a bitch! They're all awful people. They'll be keeping their eyes on you and bugging you all the time."

Hugh decided to handle the situation in his own way. Rounding up a bevy of beauties from the secretarial pool, he told them, "C'mon girls, we're all going out to lunch."

After lunch, he took them out in his station wagon to inspect the house he'd recently acquired. While most of the young ladies sashayed up and down the sidewalk in front of the house, Hugh took the others inside and showed them around.

After bringing the girls back to the office he bought a metal number plate from a hardware store. He gave the plate, bearing the number of his house, to a handyman with a hammer, tacks, and suitable instructions.

Knocking on the door of each nearby house and brandishing his hammer and number plate, the fellow would say, "From the hardware store, ma'am. Is this the house where you want these big numbers on the door?"

Hugh then told a hotel linen service that he would need weekly deliveries of sheets and towels. He gave them the number of the house across the street and asked to have their driver call to arrange the details.

"What in the world is going on over there?" asked the neighbors, as they got their heads together. "Surely no one would *dare* open a house of ill repute right here under our noses?" They formed a committee and hired an attorney to fend off the forthcoming evil.

Later, after telling the story at a cocktail party, Hugh would say, "Y'know, Joe was right. Those people next door *were* awfully stuffy. They visited me once before they learned the truth and instead of talking they'd just sit in the corner and *stare* at me."

Hugh took his new intelligence career quite seriously. But one day someone on the staff handed down a regulation saying that any CIA employee who had a conversation with a representative of the news media had to report it in full, in writing, the very next morning, no matter how unimportant it might have seemed.

It got to be an awful bother. Hugh lived next door to a newspaper publisher and three or four times a week he'd have to come to work in the morning and start off writing a note about his brief morning chat with the publisher.

Finally he wrote a memo that read like this:

7:00 P.M. Was having dinner with my wife when interrupted by low rap on front door. Investigated. Opened door and at first saw no one. Then looked down and saw Leroy, last name not available, a representative of *The Washington Post*. Conversation ran as follows:

"Hello, Leroy. How are you?"

"Fine, Mr. Troy. How you?"

"Fine, Leroy. What's the bad news?"

"Same old bad news, Mr. Troy. I come for the money."

"How much do I owe you, Leroy?"

"Two weeks, Mr. Troy."

"Here you are, Leroy."

"Thank you, Mr. Troy."

Conversation terminated. Subject Leroy disappeared down side street.

Infuriated, Hugh's superior took the memorandum to the agency's top-level staff meeting. The agency's director read it carefully and then, unable to contain himself, exploded with laughter and toppled backward in his chair. That was the last of the regulation.

To get a true idea of how Hugh loved to see phonies, stuffed shirts, and tin martinets cut down to size, consider this story he told on himself.

A friend who ranked very high in the State Department asked him over to lunch one day and Hugh dressed to the nines, including vest and homburg. At luncheon's end, his friend graciously offered to have him chauffeured home in a State Department Cadillac.

Hugh was settled comfortably in the back seat when the limousine stopped for a red light beside a load of touring high school students from Texas. Everybody on board was festooned with Pinocchio hats and plumes and sat sunken gum-deep in apple candy. One young man displayed a water pistol.

Spotting the silkhat-black Cadillac, he squirted a tentative trickle of water on the front windshield and enjoyed all the giggles.

The chauffeur looked around at Hugh as if to say: "Are you going to let him get away with a thing like that?"

Hugh adjusted his homburg, swung the back door open ponderously, leveled a forefinger at the students, and orated: "I happen to be Senator Radiant J. Lungburst of Texas, and if you hooligans are representative of the young men and women of Texas today, then it is time for our great state to hang its head in infamous shame."

The students were shocked into silence at the sight of the enraged dignitary who confronted them. But the genetic residue of Davy Crockett and Sam Houston suddenly sparked alive within the gunman. He let "Senator Lungburst" have it full stream — all over the vest, the fine worsted suit, the silk shirt, the homburg, and flush in the mush.

As the light changed, Hugh, dripping from homburg to bluchers, was still blustering at the top of his lungs: "You — you — I'll take this to the Legislature — I'll take this into the halls of the United States Senate itself. I'll . . . ."

Hugh kept yowling, bystanders kept hooting, and the boys and girls cheered their deadeye outrider as the light changed and the duel became history.

"It was perfectly wonderful," Hugh recalled. "Perfectly wonderful! You know, that kid will be a hero as long as he lives. He may grow up to be a wife beater, a snooker player, a lushwell, a dun dodger, a church shirker, and an absolute leech on the welfare and good name of the community. But as long as he lives, he'll be remembered as the guy that put that pompous old ass in his place back in Washington, D.C. that day."

Through his friend in the State Department, Hugh found that many diplomats no longer thought of writing their own speeches; they used ghost writers. In fact, he discovered that even a president of Cornell had made a speech cribbed in part from an article written for an educational journal by another university president.

At the same time, the artist had made many friends who kept bothering him for help with their paintings. Being a softie at heart, in no time he found himself doing most of the work except the signature. Logically, he put the two ideas together. Composing the following ad, and using his new address — he and Pat had recently moved — he inserted it in *The Washington Post*:

Too busy to paint?   Call on:
THE GHOST PAINTERS
1410 35th St., N.W.   Phone MI 2574
WE PAINT IT — YOU SIGN IT!
Primitive (Grandma Moses Type)
Impressionist, Modern, Cubist
Persian, Abstract
WHY NOT GIVE AN EXHIBITION?

"All I wanted to do," said Hugh, "was to crystallize editorial comment on the ghosting trend, to provoke a lot of thought on the morality of it, how far one should go. Although I had placed my own phone number on the ad, I didn't expect any replies. So I didn't tell Mrs. Troy about the ad.

"But the weirdest thing happened. The phone started to ring. People wanted to know more details.

"Then a doctor came to the door. 'I saw your ad in the paper,' he said. 'All the other doctors in my clinic are quite good at art. They send their paintings off to the doctors' art show every year. Now I want something rather small, about *so* big, just a still life of a fish and a pineapple. But don't make it too good because next year I want you to paint me something much better so my friends can see I'm improving.' I told him I'd take care of him sometime but to come back later when I wasn't so busy."

Soon more orders started pouring in. Hugh turned them all down, saying, "Sorry, but we're swamped with work." Journalists hearing of it saw a scoop. The wire service teletypes then began rattling off such disclosures as: "After thriving quietly for three years in New York, a fantastic new wrinkle in the art world, ghost painting, has moved to the nation's capital because of important new clients high in the government."

Quoting an anonymous spokesman, the stories went on to tell how the Ghost Painters, successful commercial artists in real life, were now opening a branch in Washington and were fattening up on commissions from executives who wanted to impress their friends or simply dabble in the artists and models' life.

Papers with stiff-necked editors deplored the chicanery of the deceitful new racket. Their editorials denounced the soft American underbelly of corruption in which ghost writing and ghost painting had been born. The *London Times* followed suit. In a long editorial, it deplored the unfortunate new trend in American art. "It's just another of the many growing evils that beset their society," it said, in effect. "Enough fakes bedevil the art world without more being mass-produced on such a cheap, tawdry basis. It's a reflection of the obsessive American striving for status and prestige. Thank God England has not stooped so low."

But other papers took it light-heartedly, including the *Washington Daily News* which published a painting by the "Number One Ghost" under the headline:

THAT AIN'T SPIRIT IN YOUR PAINTINGS — THAT'S GHOST!

Beseiged by correspondents, Hugh told each one that he would tell him the whole story if he would not use his name. Lie after lie bubbled up in Hugh's brain. He told reporters he was having labor troubles with his New York outfit; it was hard to find good cubists any more. Also, several of his clients, he said, had become famous artists and the Ghost Painters who had done the painting for them were getting irritable because they had to remain anonymous.

"I know what we're doing is wrong," said Hugh, putting on a repentant look. "Absolutely immoral. Once they start coming to us, they can never stop. We work so their paintings show gradual improvement. The client's first painting is really just a preview of the masterpieces to come. With each painting he shows additional talent. It's a terrible situation.

"We already have nearly forty customers, some of whom are confirmed addicts. It's puzzling. I think it has something to do with the unstable frame of mind here in Washington. This type of ghost work is a sad commentary on America. Pick up your papers. Look at the advertisements. People will write you short stories, novels, doctors' theses, anything.

"But it's a wonderful way to pick up change. It's also a fascinating sidelight on human beings. Look at our clients. The fact that they're

*"The Washington News published
a painting by the Number
One Ghost . . ."*

really cheating doesn't bother them at all. They're that unscrupu-
lous. They want fame. That's all there is to it.

"The incredible thing is that we actually change our clients' lives.
They've always dreamed about being artists. Now suddenly they
are. They have prestige, a sense of belonging. People want that so
much today, they'll stoop to anything.

"We hope you blast us in your papers. We'd welcome being
denounced. If ghosting is now part of the art world, what will be
next? What about music? Where will this business cease? It's high
time we decided."

After the first spate of news about the Ghost Painters, however,

Washington correspondents began receiving edgy queries from their New York offices. The excited gaiety of the early dispatches gave way to groans as the truth dawned. One by one, in messages such as the following, preserved in the files of the *Washington Post*, the news syndicates confessed they'd been had:

WE ARE WITHDRAWING STORY ON GHOST PAIN-
TERS WHICH WE ASKED TO BE HELD OVER LAST
NIGHT FOR FURTHER CHECKING. SOURCE HAS
REPUTATION OF BEING PRACTICAL JOKER.

Though his work with the CIA was classified, Hugh dropped occasional hints that he had to travel to other parts of the world. On his journeys to Ithaca to see his father, who was still living with the Zeissigs, he would allude to his visits to Japan, South America, and other countries.

His trips back to his old home ended in 1953 when the Zeissigs moved to Mountainside, New Jersey, Dr. Zeissig having found a more lucrative position there. Hugh's father then sold the Oak Avenue house and went with them. The professor was then 85 and, because of cataracts, was slowly going blind. "But," as Hugh remarked to a friend, "his old bean is still crystal clear and his memory goes way back to the first electric light on the campus and the first horseless carriage."

Despite his CIA work and his travels, Hugh found time to moonlight. In his trips around Washington, he had become fascinated with the city's many monuments. For over a year, their interesting histories formed the basis for a thrice-weekly column in *The Washington Post* by one "Cutler Wholecloth." "I chose that pseudonym," Hugh explained, "as the CIA objected to its spies writing for publication." He also kept his pen busy, illustrating two children's books for his Ithaca friend, Ruth Sawyer Durand: *The Enchanted Schoolhouse,* and *The Year of the Christmas Dragon.*

During his travels, Hugh had made the acquaintance of the ace British humorist and author, Stephen Potter, for whom he felt a certain kinship. For, in writing his many books, *Gamesmanship, Oneupmanship, Lifemanship,* and *Sense of Humor,* Potter had actually compiled a course in the art of winning by putting the other fellow down, a good gamesman always being "one up." With a spare frame of medium height, dark hair, and piercing, dark eyes, Potter was a wiry, intense man. Polished and voluble, he was a master of repartee.

Now Hugh found that the author was planning an American lecture tour in 1955 with stops in New York for visits with his publisher, Bennett Cerf of Random House, a radio show with Clifton Fadiman and Henry Morgan, a ball game at the Polo Grounds with Walter Cronkite, and an appearance on Dave Garroway's *Today Show.* Hugh and Pat invited him to be their guest during his stay in Washington.

"Superb welcome from the Troys this evening," the Britisher noted in his diary before his Washington lecture. "Hugh taller than ever, tenderly shining, like some eolithic dawn, softly mad, insinuatingly looming. Pat, his wife, makes one of those glorious speeches to me, beginning, 'If you only knew how much . . . . ' This sort of thing warms me up for a week. The Troys are perfectly interested, perfectly appreciative, perfectly helpful; and Hugh's marvelous stories have to be coaxed out of him."

The Englishman had just finished his Washington lecture when, as he wrote later *(Potter On America),* "it was question time. I saw Hugh getting up. I had particularly told him not to come. This Washington gamesman is the American who has raised the term 'practical joke' to a height so Olympian that a new name of greater dignity must be invented for it, a Trojan joke. He had sailed in,

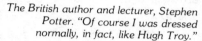
The British author and lecturer, Stephen Potter. "Of course I was dressed normally, in fact, like Hugh Troy."

looking, with his great height, like a figurehead of Neptune on the prow of a ship.

"Now he rose with the mien and voice of Captain Ahab and said, 'Would the lecturer please tell us why he is appearing in costume?' Laughter and applause. Of course I was dressed normally, in fact, like Hugh Troy, and that was the point, so it was difficult to answer. I half scrambled it, half did it clean: 'It is surely considered proper, when visiting foreign countries, to follow the customs of the aborigines.'"

So many in Hugh's circle wanted to meet his guest that he decided to have two successive cocktail parties. He then anguished over who were to be first-nighters and who second-nighters. That figured out, he then gave each guest suitable instructions.

Each of the first-nighters came in bearing a copy of a Stephen

Potter book.

"Stephen," said Hugh, "meet my good friend, John Gordon."

"Nice to meet you, John," said Potter, staring at the book in Gordon's hand, a copy of *Gamesmanship*. Following a habit developed over the years, he tentatively reached for his pen, expecting his new friend would ask him to autograph it. But John didn't mention it; he simply laid it on the piano.

"Oh, Stephen," said Hugh, shake hands with my old buddy, Dan Whitney."

"Dan, good to know you," said Potter, his eye on the copy of *Oneupmanship* in Whitney's hand. Again he reached for his pen. But Dan carried the book away and placed it on a table as Hugh was introducing the next guest. One after another they came, bringing more of the Englishman's books and dropping them around the room without saying a word about them.

Potter took the bait. Eying the disheveled heaps of books, his smile of sociability became strained, giving way to a puzzled frown. Only as the evening wore on did he catch on. By the time everyone had left he was completely relaxed and roaring at Hugh's marvelous ploy.

On the second night, the first guest to arrive, a young matron, headed immediately for the Englishman saying, "Oh, Mr. Potter, I've so enjoyed all your books. Won't you please autograph this one for me?"

Flattered, Potter took the book, reached for his pen, turned the flyleaf, and found the title, *Upland Game and Gunning*, by E. Runcey Potter. Not wishing to embarrass the woman, the author signed it with an indistinct scrawl. By this time a second guest had entered. Like the woman, he greeted the humorist with warm words of praise and handed him a Potter book to sign: *The Lower Ganges Revisited*, by Cokely Atherwart Potter, Bart. Again, somewhat testily, the Englishman scribbled something in it. On they came, more guests, each bearing a book: *I Was An Undercover*

Beatnik, by Rock Potter; *The Cumulous Blade of Being,* by Cleanth Welstone Potter; *Old Morocco Flesh-Mart Excavations,* by Dr. Ali Potter-Amir, and so on.

"Oh," said Hugh to the Britisher as he introduced the last guest, "here is another good friend that wants very much to meet you, Phil Herzbrun."

"How do you do, Phil," said Potter.

"I must apologize," said Herzbrun. "I happened to come in during the rush last night and missed meeting you. I didn't know you were the famous author. So I came again tonight to meet you and bring this book of yours." He thrust a pea-green textbook into the Englishman's hands.

"I've had it for years but never dreamed that some day I might meet the man who wrote it. Would you please autograph it for me?"

"Delighted," said Potter. Grabbing his pen, he flipped the book open. It was *Elizabethan Poetry and Prose,* by Nelson Potter. With a long-suffering glance at Hugh, he laboriously signed, "Nelson Potter, M.A." he had saved face, stroke for stroke.

Twelve

When Russia cruelly invaded and subjugated Hungary in 1956, many refugees fled to America. Learning that some of the fugitives were arriving in Washington, Hugh and Pat were among the first to rush to their aid with food and clothes. They also helped them get in touch with relatives in this country. As Hugh told his friends, "These poor people need everything, and they need it now."

By December of that year, the Troys had spent every spare cent on the unfortunates. "That was the Christmas," remembers Fran, "that Hugh and Pat, lacking funds for the usual presents, had sent me and many others small, gold-painted ceramic hearts, each about three inches high. They had made those 'hearts of gold' as a last resort. They knew we would understand."

When Hugh was approaching his tenth year in Washington, he received a letter from his old New York roommate, Bob Lent. In his reply, Hugh intimated he might leave the CIA.

Dear Bob:

Most heart-warming to hear from you and know that Houston and Rice are basking in your effervescent glow. Golly, wish we'd kept up the lines all these years so we could have seen you here last year. But let's hope for next time.

It's many a moon indeed since our last reunion with Pat's family in Ithaca. Even that damned war seems like a

159

most distant dream. We lived in Garrison on the Hudson directly across from West Point in a fabulous mountain retreat for about five years after the war, free-lance writing and a few large mural commissions. Then some folks who were getting the Central Intelligence Agency started here in Washington persuaded us to come down here to assist in establishing some odd things.

It was like having someone give me, at middle age, the chance to see a most curious other world right on this one, occupy it, and learn about it. But it's been a drain on the old bean and carcass, what's left of them. So I finally set the schedule for ten years of this; and, as soon as I can train some replacement, I'm going to set out being myself again. Just where and what, Pat and I haven't decided as yet.

I'm illustrating a book for Viking to be published next fall; and I'm sort of looking around in the more gentle atmospheres, if any, that exist. A few days last week in New York were enough to convince me that the atmosphere we created at 8 West 76th Street requires a millionaire's stipend to maintain there today . . . .

I'm very tempted to accept an invitation from this year's senior class at Cornell to engage in a sort of evening with them wondering out loud how's it's possible to have fun any more . . . .

Pat recalls our pleasant visit with you, and joins in our very best, Bob. Don't you need a very abstract mural in something you're up to? I've got one just bustin' out all over.

Affectionately,
Hugh

Hugh did accept the invitation of Cornell's class of 1960 mentioned in his letter to Bob. From his note to the class secretary:

> Your thoughtful arrangements for our visit sound fine.
> Meeting you and seeing old friends on the campus as you
> outline, most heartwarming. And particularly this
> chance to meet the active, creative gentlemen of the
> undergraduate sphere . . . .

One of those "creative gentlemen" was Bob Mayers, then on the
staff of Cornell's radio station WVBR who taped Hugh's talk to the
class for a later broadcast. Hugh, who had been billed as "Cornell's
Only Living Legend," was more interested in seeing and hearing the
present state of campus humor than he was in retelling his famous
anecdotes.

The audience of over two hundred couldn't seem to get enough
of Hugh's stories. The printed word cannot convey his many nuan-
ces of tone and emotion or reproduce the tidal waves of laughter
that punctuated his remarks and often drowned out his words. He
didn't have time, of course, to relate many of his most enjoyable
tales.

But he did tell how he duped Professor Pa Martin with his "fallen
ceiling," how he supposedly got a ten-dollar gold piece for a dime,
how he punched his own IBM card while being inducted into the
service, and how he wrote the folk tales of old Saipan.

He also told the group of the prank he played on President Tru-
man's Secretary of State, Dean Acheson:

> This incident took place, as I recall, toward the end of
> the Truman administration. Dean Acheson looks more
> like a Secretary of State than anyone else could ever
> hope to look. With his erect, military bearing, and bristly,
> sandy, adjutant's mustache, the Secretary was the prot-
> otype of the starch-straight, dignified, professional

diplomat.

Dean and his children, who I knew quite well, didn't live far from my place. Their home was near a Presbyterian church on P Street that all the staid old Republican ladies attended every Sunday morning. Acheson didn't live there all the time; he had another house in the country.

One weekend it happened that the Secretary was at his country house. His children were in town, though, and helped me work this out. First, we hired a character actor of about Acheson's build. Then we togged him out in Dean's morning coat, his striped pants, his silk hat — the whole works that Acheson had to wear whenever he met a visiting dignitary at the airport.

So, on this particular Sunday morning, when the prim and proper old Republican ladies trooped by the Secretary's charming home in Georgetown, there, sitting on the front steps, was Dean Acheson in his full morning regalia, *fishing*. In a little pail of water.

His kids and I were sitting at a friend's house across the street, enjoying the show and especially the remarks of the passersby. As one group of dowagers slowed down to look at the spectacle with their mouths open, we could hear them saying,

"Dear, dear, isn't it sad?"

"Why, the poor man. He's off his rocker."

"Oh, my. They'll have to come and take him away."

The first of April is a day many of us set aside to play more or less amiably asinine tricks on our neighbors. The tradition persists and, for proof, you can check with any zoo keeper. On April Fool's Day gullible dupes will ring his phone and explain that Mr. Fox or Miss Ellie Phant left word to call. Even people who run casket factories have been caught in the middle. The jokers leave word for you to call a certain telephone number to check on "a box being held for you."

But is such foolishness ever paraded before a whole nation? Yes, it did happen once in Washington when Dave Garroway, the popular host of the *Today Show*, asked Hugh Troy to appear as a guest one morning.

Dave wasn't there; Faye Emerson was taking his place. She and the orchestra leader, Skitch Henderson, had just been divorced in nationally headlined court proceedings. A mutual friend introduced Hugh to Miss Emerson as, "Mr Troy, the head of a new federal division, the Department Forum." Miss Emerson was a little puzzled.

"Mr. Troy, your new division sounds interesting. Just what are its aims and purposes?"

"I'm very glad you asked that question, Mrs. Henderson. Our philosophy is founded on the bedrock of good old American enterprise in its finest tradition. We will keep our eyes unwaveringly on that bright star that symbolizes our number one goal, the improvement of our foreign relations, especially our foreign trade. The way we have been mishandling our foreign relations is simply disgraceful.

"Our foreign trade is our lifeblood, Mrs. Henderson. Why, we have let a bunch of striped-pants, blundering bureaucrats throw it into a shambles. Most of them are permanently glued to their swivel chairs. They don't know what it means to get off their duffs and work for an honest dollar, Mrs. Henderson."

Miss Emerson stiffened. "It's *Miss Emerson,* not Mrs. Henderson."

"Oh, excuse me. As I was saying, in this new division we'll throw all our moldy old methods in the ash can. Our foreign representatives will be experienced free enterprisers. We'll use businessmen abroad instead of these Harvard diplomats.

"Take Africa for a good example, Mrs. Henderson. That whole

"Dave Garroway, host of the Today Show, asked Hugh to appear as a guest one morning."

continent is just one big piece of mismanaged real estate. Zechendorf, the real estate financier, could straighten things out there in a hurry.

"We needn't be ashamed of admitting that we want to make money, Mrs. Henderson. In fact, we should be proud of it. Every one of our new businessman representatives will wear a small gold dollar sign in his lapel as a sign of our new philosophy.

"Big corporations could be a fine source of new manpower for this program, Mrs. Henderson. In fact, the corporations should bid for the foreign service jobs. Besides representing America, our men could rake in plenty for themselves so we wouldn't have to pay them a cent. You see, Mrs. Henderson, we could make money for the government instead of draining the taxpapers."

Infuriated by Hugh's insistence on calling her "Mrs. Henderson," and overwhelmed for a moment by the impact of Hugh's ideas, Miss Emerson tried to collect her thoughts.

"But, Mr. Troy, isn't it possible that your new system would lead to immense profits for some concerns? Might it not get out of hand, make a lot of millionaires, and cause a big scandal?" She looked worried.

But her concern didn't last long. Hugh's friend stepped up.

"I see we're running out of time. Don't be worried, Miss Emerson. There is no new division. Mr. Troy's first name is Hugh. As you may recall, he is known as America's leading practical joker. And . . . oh, yes . . . this is April Fool's Day."

Hugh's hoax on the *Today Show* may have been his last contribution to the annals of humorous deception. In addition to retiring from the CIA, he apparently retired gracefully from the world of trickery, content to let the years roll by during a leisurely life of writing and painting. His old crony, Walt Nield, was in touch with him then.

Walt spent a few days with Pat and Hugh in Georgetown in the winter of 1960. He found them very domestic and having fun decorating their new place at 2531 Q St., N.W. In the garden, a delightful, tiny, walled-in area, was a set of three old iron folding chairs in a straight line. Discreetly lettered on the chair backs was this inscription:

RESERVED FOR   THE GENERAL   AND PARTY

In the library was an unfinished, but framed, triptych that Hugh was working on. From ten feet away, it looked like a religious work from the Fifteenth Century. It had grown out of a conversation between Hugh and Pat during the war, when it was feared that Rome would be bombed.

It was thought that Pope Pius might have to flee the city and even seek haven in the United States. At that time Pat wondered how the Pope would travel. "Why," replied Hugh, "by papal submarine, of course." From that incident, Hugh got the idea for the triptych.

The first panel depicted the Vatican under siege and the Pope being alerted by angels. In the background is Saint Peter's cathedral being blown apart by falling bombs.

In the second panel, President Roosevelt is sending a submarine to rescue the Pope. In the third, the mission is successful and the sub is sailing away from Italy on its way to Brooklyn. Pius XII is peering through a periscope of the tiny submarine.

The panels were done in the authentic manner of the Fifteenth Century religious painter, Fra Angelico, and signed "Fra Hugh." Pat kept them on the piano in fretted gilt frames.

The fall of 1962 found Walt Nield in the hospital. In Hugh's letter to Walt, we find the first intimation that Hugh had been in the hospital too:

> Dear Walter:
>
> When I tried to reach you by phone just now, the lady said she couldn't call you. I recall so well your telling me how wonderful it was to be in that ward at Columbia Medical Center. Hope you are in one with as interesting folk as that particular man you described to us. Guess I told you that when I was at Walter Reid, the fabulous people in my ward impressed themselves sharply on my memory, although we had to see some depart each A.M. to have a limb chopped off.
>
> I couldn't quite get just what has you in the hands of the proper people. I hope it is a festering corn or bunion, the kind of trouble we don't talk about. It seems to be excusable to talk about adhesions but, as Emily Post states in her opus, "Never say, 'My feet hurt.' "
>
> She suggests it might be polite to say, "My left foot hurts," or "My right foot hurts." I've arrived at a solution, used now since age 50, "My left foot hurts and my right foot hurts." No plain old tired feet for me!
>
> Walter, I think of you so very often. All the most cherished folk seem to be so scattered over the globe. Not just by distance, time and space, but by inclination and circumstance.

Pat, whom I talked to a few minutes ago, sends best and love.

Walter, may all be well with you and all Nields.

Fondest thoughts,
Hugh

A year later, Hugh was again in the hospital, this time for a longer stay. He explains in this letter to his fellow-Cornellian, Red Woodin:

Dear Red:

Since hearing from you I've been tied down by some elusive bugs or would have written you sooner. I'm presently ensconced in the very fine George Washington University Hospital for a couple weeks or so posing for innumerable interior views and letting the white-coated gentry ride roughshod over my pallid hunt country.

There's a most amusing and famous surgeon here, Dr. Charles Wise, who is quite a wag. He has real butterflies show up in the X-ray pictures of his patients' stomachs, and little men with sledge hammers working away inside skull X-rays.

My own wonderful doctor got so mad at a bitchy woman patient who refused to pay him after a long series of expensive tests he made on her insistence and could find nothing wrong, he turned the bill over to the A.M.A. collection agency. When she started to pay in small dribbles, she wrote him to say that he owed her a "diagnosis" of her ailment for her money.

He wrote her this letter and hopes she sues him:

Dear Mrs. Blank:

You're fat.

Yours truly,
Charles W. Thompson, M.D.

Didn't mean this note to be so full of "jolly" hospital lore. Hope you and Mrs. Woodin are in these environs before long. There's lots to talk about.

And thanks so much for thinking of me.

Very best wishes,
Hugh

During the year following his letter to Woodin, Hugh apparently became morose, withdrawn, despondent over his continuing ill health. By the summer of 1964 there was only one possible end to his steadily worsening condition. Strangely, he appeared to recognize this and seemed reconciled to it. Before he died, on July 8th, at fifty-eight, he phoned many of those he was close to during his Cornell days. Among those he called was Dave Davis in Connecticut.

"When I took the call," said Dave, "I didn't recognize Hugh's voice at first. When I did, I felt flattered because we had been out of touch for thirty years. He talked quite a while to my wife, Mary, and me. As I listened, a strange feeling came over me. I understood he was trying to say, 'Farewell' and had made similar calls to others."

So, at the end, Hugh was not thinking of himself. As he had countless times in the past, Hugh was thinking only of his old, old friends.

"Hugh Troy? Sure, I remember . . ."

This epilog offers a few glimpses of the famous prankster by his intimates. (Class year is noted for Cornellians.)

Bob Abbott: He dragged me to a Greenwich Village night club to see a short, fat lady coloratura who sang an involved operatic aria while she folded a huge sheet of paper into small squares and tore away bits of it with dramatic flourishes, all in tempo, until, at her grand finale, she unfurled a beautiful design in Spanish lace. He *loved* her! Night after night he went back to catch her act and to lead the applause, yelling, "Bravo! Bravo! Bravo!"

Stew Beecher '26: I still have the note he sent me after my father died: "Dear Stew: I imagine you are in a pretty unsettled state of mind right now and that anything I can say would be inane. But, you see, this is the time when I realize there is a bond between us and I must write to you . . . ."

Mrs. Morris Bishop: We were coming home from a movie in Ithaca in his old Model T when he said he was having trouble getting up University Avenue hill. We shuddered to a stop, then rolled down the hill backwards. That was Hugh—always trying strange things just to get your reaction.

Mary Fuertes Boynton '31: "When I was walking down the hill to school," Hugh said, "I saw, in the second-floor window of a house on Buffalo Street, a sign saying PINKING DONE HERE. I wonder what it means. It sounds wicked."

George Bryon '30: Hugh asked Daisy Farrand, wife of Cornell's

169

president, if she would like to join us for dinner at our fraternity house, telling her to expect a surprise. She accepted. Our waiter first brought us pie, then, in turn, potatoes, steak, salad, hors d'oeuvres, and soup.

Hunt Bradley '26: At a dance at our fraternity house, Hugh gave a string of imitation pearls to a girl friend about to leave on a round-the-world cruise. During the dance, while the pearls hung around her neck, he managed to break the string. We stopped the dance, gave her all the pearls we could find, and she left for her trip. Hugh had her itinerary. Waiting for her at each of her hotels in London, Paris, Rome, and Tokyo was a pearl with a note from Hugh saying the boys had just found it.

Erling Brauner '29: One of Hugh's friends came home one night, opened his door, and snapped the light switch. A blinding blaze of light flooded the room which then went dark. Hugh had filled the sockets with flash bulbs.

Fred Emmons '28: At Cornell I had a blind date with a girl from out Cortland way. Having just returned to America from a Swiss finishing school, she was presumed to be very sophisticated. The next day a man phoned me and asked what my intentions were toward his innocent little daughter. He grilled me severely and left me terribly confused. It was some time before I found out it was Hugh who had called me.

Arlene Francis: Hugh had loaned me a paper I had to return so while in his neighborhood I went up to his apartment. To my surprise, his door bore a large sign: MEASLES. So, instead of knocking I pushed my paper through his mail slot and started to leave. But suddenly Hugh opened his door. His face was disfigured by scores of telltale red spots.

"Why, Hugh," I stammered. "I—I'm so sorry. I'd better go." And I hurried to the stairs.

"Arlene!" he said. "Oh, don't mind that sign. Come on in."

"But your—your face," I cried.

"Oh, heck," he laughed, "that's only finger paint."

Paul Gurney '27: Hugh helped plan a reception in his home for a visiting professor. Because their guest was interested in avant-garde art, Hugh replaced some of the pictures on the walls with new ones: collages of food items glued in place. One was kosher pickles, olives, and rye bread spread with limburger; a second, baby shoes, a nippled bottle, and radishes; a third, clock works with banana peels and mashed potato. They were all greatly admired and discussed, especially the fourth: gravy on a necktie with a sardine stickpin.

Julian Everett '25. A large gas meter and its pipework I remember in the hall of Hugh's New York apartment was an eyesore. The next time I saw it, Hugh had added more pipes made with cardboard mailing tubes, still more painted on the wall, and had painted the meter and pipes in different colors. *Voila!* A work of art!

John Gatling '28: After my wife, Eleanor, and I had climbed to the top deck of a Fifth Avenue bus, I saw Hugh and a friend sitting up front. I wanted to hail him. But he was telling his companion a hair-raising story that had all the riders leaning forward, straining to hear him. Most of his words were low-key but now and then I'd catch a loud phrase like, "And then I bit her ear off." We left later without spoiling his act.

Don Hershey '27: Professor Frazer asked each one in our architecture class to give him, within forty-eight hours, a drawing, a conception of what a brightly floodlighted hydroelectric plant might look like at night. Though Hugh was overloaded with other work, he got his drawing in on time. It was a canvas showing a large, solid black rectangle titled, *Hydroelectric Plant At Night (Fuse blown)*.

Karl Kellerman '29: Al Smith, ex-governor of New York, once invited Hugh to a dance party in his apartment at One Fifth Avenue. "Al," said Hugh, "may I bring my sister-in-law, Denise?" "By all means," said Al. "I'd love to meet her." Hugh brought her through the reception line where Al shook her hand. She was a mannikin I had helped Hugh carry in.

Ruth Tompkins Lott '30: In November, 1930 I appeared in a play in Cornell's Willard Straight theater then was surprised to receive a wire: PLEASED WITH PERFORMANCE. GRACE AND I SEND GREETINGS. CALVIN COOLIDGE.

Bob Mayers '59: In his talk to Cornell students in 1960, Hugh told how he entered a subway car carrying, under his coat, a false leg wearing a silk stocking and lady's shoe. After taking his seat, he slowly dropped the leg between his own legs. "It bothered nearby passengers so much," said Hugh, "that they got up and walked away."

Valerie Nield Mitchell: As a young girl, I almost believed him when he told me that his wife, Pat, did up her hair with an egg beater. He taught me to play tunes on wine glasses with wet fingers. There should be an "Uncle Hugh" in every child's life.

Virginia Gray Moxley: While driving near Garrison, N.Y., I had a flat tire. Along came my neighbor, Hugh Troy, who offered to take me and my two sons home. As we rode along, the boys started acting up. "Keep quiet and sit down," I told them. "Listen , boys, " said Hugh, "you can jump and scream all you want to. If your mother says another word, I'll put her out of the car."

Walt Nield '27: Hugh's friends would occasionally encounter him on a street corner or train platform "reading" a Chinese newspaper.

On my birthday in 1941 my children gave me a party. Hugh came early and installed under our table a tin can with a rosined string attached to one end. When he pulled the string, the tin can made a roar. He explained, "We're now eating on a 'groaning board'."

Herm Redden '27: At Cornell, Hugh was riding a bike in front of Willard Straight Hall when he spied a big sedan at the curb. Mama and Papa, followed by three young girls, got out, each one greeting in turn a freshman on the sidewalk, Hugh stopped, got in the car on the road side, crawled through and out, then shook hands with the astonished freshman.

Hilda Berry Sanford: My father, Romeyn Berry '04, had arranged for Hugh to paint a scene on a large window in the Johnny Parsons Club, formerly on Cornell's Beebe Lake. One day, as a young girl, I was watching him at work. At his direction I changed the rolls on a player piano we were listening to. He complained, however, that the music sounded monotonous. So he had me unwind one of the rolls, rewind it backwards, and play it. It was a weird but refreshing change.

One winter, no snow had fallen by Christmas eve so the Catholic church in downtown Ithaca was packed for midnight Mass. Hugh and a friend came in very late, with their hair and clothes covered with a half-inch of snow. They kept brushing it off as they stamped down the center aisle to a pew in front.

Murmurs of surprise and alarm ran through the congregation for many foresaw trouble driving back up to their homes on East Hill. But, when they left the church, they found the ground perfectly clear. Hugh had covered his friend and himself with *artificial* snow.

Fran Troy '29: The trolley to the Ithaca railroad station ran right past our house. One day Hugh stood near the tracks as the trolley came along. As the motorman stopped the car, Hugh put one foot on the step and tied his shoe lace. "Thanks very much," he said to the motorman as he walked away. "Just needed a place to rest my foot."

Harry Wade '26: He nearly turned friends away from my wedding. He was one of my ushers and, as each guest came through the door, Hugh asked him, "Would you like a four or five dollar seat?"

Edith Cuervo Zeissig '30: At more than one party the host would introduce Hugh to a guest. The guest would extend his hand and find himself grasping a large iron hook sticking out of Hugh's sleeve. "Glad to meet you," Hugh would say. "Pardon the hook."

Emile J. Zimmer, Jr. '26: I knew Hugh well and will always remember how he faithfully visited my widowed mother in New York. He kept her howling with laughter each time. She *loved* his visits.

Swapping Tales of Hugh Troy*

Cornell accomplices and friends of Hugh Troy swap stories of the great trickster. Left to right: Paul Gurney '26, cartoonist, who helped Hugh set up his "poor baby brother" deception; Walt Nield '27, Hugh's lifelong friend; Don Hershey '27, Hugh's confederate in his "fallen ceiling" and "walking statues" stunts; Hal Frincke '28, who helped Hugh in his "freshman class picture" prank; author Con Troy; Hunt Bradley '26, Hugh's helper in his "Ducks in the Organ" hoax; columnist Betty Troy (the book was her idea), George Siebenthaler '27, who helped Hugh corral freshmen for their "class picture." The sign carries an early version of the title for the book.

*Taken in Sibley Hall, Cornell University, June, 1977.

175

Biographical Notes

In 1852 the first Hugh Troy left Ireland for America and settled on a farm near Ithaca, N. Y., the home of Cornell University. His grandson, the second Hugh Troy, graduated from Cornell in 1895, married an Irish girl, Mary Wall, then became the university's professor of dairy chemistry. The third Hugh Troy, the subject of our narrative, was born on April 28, 1906, the second of three children.

Hugh showed his artistic talent in 1922 when he produced a full page illustration for his Ithaca High School yearbook. Later, in Cornell, he drew a cover in color and a dozen cartoons for the student magazine, the *Widow,* also two full page plates for the 1925 yearbook. That work helped prepare him for his career as a muralist.

Regrettably, very little of his mural work exists in its original state. The work of a muralist, like that of many artists, is perishable. It decorates walls which may be covered over, altered, or even torn down. Below is only a partial list of buildings in which Hugh Troy executed murals in his own name.

1. Heigh-Ho Club, New York.
2. Toffenetti Restaurant, New York.
3. Savoy Plaza Hotel, New York.
4. 1939 World's Fair Swift and French pavilions.
5. Ambassador Hotel, Washington, D.C.
6. Roger Smith Hotel, Washington. D.C.
7. Atlanta (Ga.) Public Library
8. Mark Twain Hotel, Elmira, N.Y.
*9. Ithaca Hotel, Ithaca, N.Y.
*10. Ithaca Yacht Club, Ithaca, N.Y.

Those marked with an asterisk were painted on canvas or plywood and still exist. They were removed before the buildings housing them were torn down or altered.

Who really wrote *Laugh With Hugh Troy?*

Just as Vivaldi borrowed from other composers, I borrowed from hundreds who knew my cousin, Hugh Troy. So, in effect, those who really wrote this volume are:

My wife, Betty, a columnist and avid collector of Hugh Troy lore, whose newspapers, clippings, and correspondence formed a foundation for the book.

Hugh's brother, Francis, Cornell '29, a fountain of facts on Hugh's life, and Hugh's delightfully loquacious cousin, Edith Cuervo Zeissig '30.

Hugh's old buddy and admirer, Don Hershey '27, that prodigious pen-pusher, who gave my mailman lumbago with his 204 pages of letters loaded with reminiscences and names of other Hugh Troy fans.

Mary Fuertes Boynton '31, Robert J. F. Lent '26, Walter K. Nield '27, and Royal K. Woodin '49, who gave me copies of Hugh's letters.

Bob Mayers '59, who loaned me his superb tape recording of Hugh's talk to the Cornell class of 1960.

Authors Joe Bryan, III, H. Allen Smith, and Tom Wolfe, who were the first to proclaim Hugh Troy's genius.

Barrett Gallagher '36, eminent photographer and Hugh's working partner in New York, who gave me many anecdotes, sketches made by Hugh, and photographs of Hugh's murals.

Bob Abbott, Hugh's "paint boy" in New York, whose long single-spaced letters are packed with memories of his months with the jokester.

Erling Brauner '29, Karl Kellerman '29, Robert J. F. Lent '26, and Jack Powell, who were, in turn, Hugh's roommates in New York.

W. Stewart Beecher '26, Ransom S. Holmes, Jr. '27, Daniel M. C. Hopping '27, Emile J. Zimmer, Jr. '26, and Don "The Pirate" Dickerman, for their letters, photos, and literature.

Those helpful people who knew Hugh in Washington: Benjamin C. Bradlee, editor, *The Washington Post*, and Philip Herzbrun; also

Hugh's co-workers in the CIA: Finis Farr, Howard E. Hunt, and Robert C. Richardson, III.

And scores of others including these Cornellians: '24: Joseph C. Nobile   '25: Julian G. Everett, Kenneth M. Young   '26: Harry L. Alper, Hunt Bradley, David Davis, Harry I. Johnstone, Kenneth L. Washburn   '27: H. Stilwell Brown, Richard L. Masters, Herman Redden, George Siebenthaler, William J. Waters   '28: Richard G. Belcher, Harold C. Frincke, John C. Gatling, James D. Pond, Melita Taddiken, Philip Will, Jr.

'29: Robert E. Alexander, Howard Matteson, Kathryn Hannon Oldberg, Sidney Oldberg   '30: George F. Bryon, Frederick W. Short   '32: George D. Bancroft   '33: Donn E. Emmons '34: Arthur G. Odell, Jr.   '37: William S. Lydle, Jr.   '38: Frederick Hillegas   '50: Lydia Schurman Godfrey,   '80: Joey Green.

Also these non-Cornellians: Taylor G. Belcher, Alison Mason Kingsbury Bishop, Arlene Francis, Robert H. Head, Polly Bullard Holden, Elizabeth N. Loder, Virginia Gray Moxley, Valerie Nield Mitchell, Gene and Helen Rayburn, Hilda Berry Sanford, Dr. Seuss (Theodor S. Geisel), my brother, Francis H. Troy, and Rudy Vallee.

Pictorial Credits

My thanks go to these generous people for illustrations not credited elsewhere:

W. Stewart Beecher '26 for the *Globe and Square Dealer* editorial board photos in Chapter 3.

Don, "The Pirate" Dickerman, owner of the former Heigh-Ho Club, for the photo of Hugh Troy's mural in the club, Chapter 4.

Barrett Gallagher '36, who furnished the "Sidewalk Superintendent" card, Chapter 6, and who took the photo of Hugh Troy in Chapter 6, the mural design for a Catskills hotel, Chapter 7, and the Toffenetti restaurant mural, Chapter 8.

Dave Garroway for his photo, Chapter 12.

Paul Gurney '27 for his illustrations made for this book, Chapter 7.

Ransom S. Holmes, Jr., '27 for a copy of *The Globe and Square Dealer* and a copy of the *Syracuse American,* sources for the material shown in Chapter 3.

Daniel M. C. Hopping '27 for Hugh's New Year's card shown in Chapter 3.

Karl Kellerman '29 for his sketch of Troy's Thirty Acres in Chapter 5.

General Curtis LeMay for his photo, Chapter 9.

Robert J. F. Lent, '26 for the photo of the Daily News globe, Chapter 5.

D. Putnam Brinley's niece, Elizabeth N. Loder, for the photo of Hugh and the Metropolitan Life mural, Chapter 8.

William S. Lydle, Jr. '37 for the photo of Hugh Troy in the frontispiece and on the jacket.

Valerie Nield Mitchell for copies of Hugh's letters showing the "animals on Saipan," Chapter 10.

George Siebenthaler '27 for his sketch of the Dunking Tank, Chapter 2.

Francis B. Troy '29 for the illustration of part of the Savoy Plaza Hotel mural, Chapter 6.

Francis H. Troy and the Arnot Art Museum, Elmira, N.Y., for the illustration in Chapter 7 of Hugh Troy's mural in the former Mark Twain Hotel, Elmira, N.Y.

The Cornell Archives for the six photos in Chapter 1 and the photo of the "freshman class picture" hoax, Chapter 2.

The author took the pictures of the statues and footprints shown in Chapter 2, the apartment houses, Chapters 4 and 5, and Hugh's home in Garrison, N.Y., Chapter 10.

C.T.

Acknowledgments

Joe Bryan, III, Lewis B. McCabe, Jr., Scott Meredith, M.J. O'Brien, Eric Purdon, my son Jack, and especially Dan Sontup, kindly showed me ways to improve the manuscript.

For articles and photos from the Cornell archives my appreciation goes to Herbert Finch, Assistant Librarian, Kathleen Jacklin, Archivist, and the Archives staff.

John Marcham, editor, and Elsie Peterson, associate editor of Cornell Alumni News were of great help to me in contacting Cornellians who knew Hugh Troy. Others at Cornell who assisted are Frank B. Clifford, Director of Alumni Affairs, John A. Ferriss, Cornell Athletic Department, and Kermit C. Parsons, former Dean, College of Architecture, Arts and Planning.

For their help in research, my thanks go to Gunter Pohl, Director, Local History Division, New York Public Library, the Arnot Art Museum, Elmira, N.Y., and the staffs of the public libraries of Elmira, N.Y., Reading, Pa., and Wyomissing, Pa.

A number of incidents in the text are based in part on their description by Hugh Troy's friend, Ithaca's beloved author and poet, Morris Bishop, Cornell Historian, in his splendid book, *A History of Cornell*.

The public relations staff of Rockefeller Center kindly gave me useful information and permission to use the illustration of the Fountain of Youth mural shown in Chapter 6.

The quotation in Chapter 4 from *The Spaces in Between* by Nathaniel A. Owings is reprinted by permission of the publisher,

Selected Bibliography

BOOKS

Bishop, Morris. *A History of Cornell*. Ithaca, N.Y.: Cornell University Press, 1962.

Diven, Jeanette M. *Public Art in Elmira, N.Y.* Elmira: Association of Commerce, Ca. 1950.

Durand, Ruth Sawyer. *The Enchanted Schoolhouse*. New York: The Viking Press, Inc. 1956.

————. *The Year of the Christmas Dragon*. New York: The Viking Press, Inc. 1960.

Green, Joey, Ed. *Cornell Widow Hundredth Anniversary Anthology*. Ithaca, N.Y.: Cornell Widow, 1981.

Hunt, Howard E. *Undercover*. New York: G. B. Putnam's Sons, 1974.

Krinsky, Carol. *Rockefeller Center*. New York: Oxford University Press, 1978.

Owings, Nathaniel A. *The Spaces in Between*. Boston, Mass.: Houghton Mifflin Company, 1973.

Potter, Stephen. *Gamesmanship*. New York: Holt, Rinehart, and Winston, 1948.

————. *Lifemanship*. New York: Henry Holt and Co., 1951.

————. *Oneupmanship*. New York: Henry Holt and Co., 1958.

————. *Potter on America*. New York: Random House, 1957.

————. *Sense of Humor*. New York: Henry Holt and Co., 1954.

Smith, H. Allen. *Life in a Putty Knife Factory*. New York: Doubleday Doran and Co., 1943.

————. *The Compleat Practical Joker*. New York: Doubleday and Co., Inc., 1953.

————. *Poor H. Allen Smith's Almanac*. Greenwich, Conn.: Fawcett Publications Inc., 1965.

Troy, Hugh. *Maud for a Day*. New York: Oxford University Press, 1940.

————. *The Chippendale Dam*. New York: Oxford University Press, 1941.

————. *Five Golden Wrens*. New York: Oxford University Press, 1943.

Vallee, Rudy. *Let the Chips Fall*. Harrisburg, Pa.: Stackpole Books, 1975.

Wallechinsky, David, and Wallace, Irving. *The People's Almanac No. 2*. New York: William Morrow and Co., 1978.

PERIODICALS

"Art, Bathtubs, and Bald Heads." *Cornell Daily Sun*, Feb. 28, 1952.

"Bad Taste Causes Ban on Naughty Cornell Magazine." *Syracuse (N.Y.) American*, May 29, 1926.

Barber, Charles W. "Hugh Troy's Bold Images." *Elmira* (N.Y.) *Telegram*, July 19, 1964.

Bell, Barbara. "Ithaca Yachtsmen Like to Tell Tall Tales." *Ithaca* (N.Y.) *Journal*, Jan. 3, 1976.

_____ . "Of Old Sea Dogs, Wags, and Tales." *Ithaca* (N.Y.) *Journal*, Jan. 10, 1976.

"Books Written by Ithacans to be Issued." *Ithaca* (N.Y.) *Journal*, Aug. 14, 1941.

Bryan, Joe, III. "How the Report on Messhall Flypapers Started." *Richmond* (Va.) *News Leader*. Ca. 1950.

_____ . "Three Practical Jokers." *Esquire*, Vol. XIX, June 1943.

Davis, J. W. "Tomorrow's the Day—So Watch Out." *Patriot-News*, Harrisburg, Pa. March 31, 1965.

Elliot, Ian. "King of the Practical Jokers." *Herald American*, Syracuse, N.Y. July 19, 1964.

Ferris, John. "Troy Batted Out Homers." *New York World Telegram and Sun*, Sept. 23, 1958.

_____ . "Hugh Troy, Artist of the Homeric Practical Joke." *New York World Telegram*, Sept. 23, 1958.

"Former Cornellian Decorates Ivy Room." *Cornell Daily Sun*, Jan. 9, 1947.

"Funster Muralist Decorates Yacht Club." *Ithaca* (N.Y.) *Journal*, July 19, 1940.

"Goddess Minerva Returns from War to Decorate Willard Straight Ivy Room." *Cornell Alumni News*, Vol. 49, No. 12, Feb. 1, 1947.

Hancock, Elise. "The News Goes to Reunion." *Cornell Alumni News*, Vol. 75, No. 2, September, 1972.

"Hugh Troy." *The Washington Post*, July 12, 1964.

"Hugh Troy, Artist and Writer, Known as Practical Joker, Dies." *New York Times*, July 9, 1964.

"Hugh Troy, Famed Graduate, to Talk at University Today." *Cornell Daily Sun*, May 10, 1960.

Jansen, Harold. "Hugh Troy, Top Joker, Says Gags Come Easily." *Ithaca* (N.Y.) *Journal,* May 11, 1960.

Kaman, Jack, "Who's Hugh?—The Good Humor Man." *Cornell Daily Sun,* March 26, 1935.

Kane, Martin. "Practical Joke May Be the Basis for New Form of Art." *The Enid* (Okla.) *Morning News,* Aug. 23, 1940.

McKelway, St. Clair. "Hugh Troy, Perennial Undergraduate." *Cornell Widow,* Vol. 56, Oct., Nov. 1950.

Miles, William E. "Pranks for the Memory." *Elks Magazine,* Oct. 1975.

Ostermann, Robert. "The Art and the Motives in the Practical Joke—in the World's Hugh Troys, Modern Court Jesters." *National Observer,* July 27, 1964.

————. "Hugh Troy '26, Artist, Author, Unexcelled Master of the Benign Joke." *Cornell Alumni News,* Vol. 67, No. 7, Feb. 1965.

"Prize for Best Child's Book Won by Soldier." *New York Herald Tribune,* Mar. 21, 1943.

Schurman, Lydia. "That Ain't Spirit in Your Paintings—That's Ghost!" *Washington Daily News,* Feb. 9, 1952.

Simon, Caroline. "Hugh Troy Relates Pranks, Discusses Past Experiences." *Ithaca,* (N.Y.) *Journal,* May 11, 1960.

"Some Fun." *The New Yorker,* Vol. 12, May 30, 1936.

Spong, Richard. "An Historic Hoaxist." *Washington Post,* Mar. 19, 1972.

"Spring Day Paper Is Suppressed on Hill." *Ithaca* (N.Y.) *Journal,* May 24, 1926.

"Trojan Enterprise." *Time,* Vol. 59, Feb. 18, 1952.

"Trojan Horsing Around." *The New Yorker,* Vol. 16, Aug. 17, 1940.

"Troy, '26, April Fool's King." *Cornell Alumni News,* Vol. 66, No. 9, April 1964.

"Troy Completes Hotel Murals." *Elmira* (N.Y.) *Star-Gazette,* Nov. 30, 1936.

"Troy, Troy Again." *This Week Magazine,* July 16, 1961.

Troy, Hugh. "Best Wishes." *The New Yorker,* Vol. 11, Sept. 14, 1945.

————. "Cast Up by the Ocean." *Cornell Widow,* Vol. **XXX,** No. 10, April 24, 1924.

————. "Never Had A Lesson." *Esquire,* Vol. VII, June, 1937.

————. "The Impurity of Science." *Esquire,* Vol. VIII, No. 6, Dec., 1937.

Wolfe, Tom. "King of Hoaxers Deals His Jokers Like A Real Ace." *Washington Post*, Jan. 14, 1962.

_____. "The Greatest Prankster's Exploits." *New York Herald Tribune*, July 12, 1964.

Wallechinsky, David, and Wallace, Irving. "World's Greatest Practical Joker Even Hoodwinked the Pentagon." *National Enquirer*, Sept. 5, 1978.

_____. "Life Was A Gag to Hugh Troy." *Boston Sunday Globe*, Dec. 23, 1979.

Index

Abbott, Robert P., 96, 113, 169
Acheson, Dean, 161
Alexander, Robert E., 66
Ambassador Hotel, 100
America House, 138
"Architects' House," 24
Army Air Corps, 117, 124
Artists' Ball, 66
Arts Quad, Cornell, 14
Atlanta Public Library, 176

Bailey Hall, Cornell, 109
Baldwin's Fish Market, 73
Barnes, Fred, 53
Barnes Hall, 45
Barton Hall, Cornell, 86
Baruch, Bernard, 82
Beebe Lake, 22
Beecher, W. Stewart, 52, 169
Berry, Romeyn, 49
Bishop, Morris, Mrs., 169
Boothroyd, Samuel L., 46
Boyle's Thirty Acres, 72
Boynton, Mary Fuertes, 169
Bradley, Hunt, 170, 175
Brauner, Erling B., 68, 170
Brinley, D. Putnam, 68, 105
Brown, H. Stilwell, 21
Bryan, Joe, III, 145
Bryant, Laura, 142
Bryon, George, 169
Byrd Field, 119

Carroll, Lewis, 92, 102
Central Intelligence Agency, 145, 160
Central Park, New York, 61
Cerf, Bennett, 154
Chambord Restaurant, 100
Chaplin, Charles, 13
Charette meetings, 27
Chippendale Dam, The, 110, 139

*Connecticut Yankee, A, in King
    Arthur's Court,* 91
Connecticut Yankees, The, 57
Coolidge, Calvin, 13
Consolidated Edison Co., 59
Cornell Daily Sun, 46-8
Cornell, Ezra, 13, 24, 36-7
Cornell, Katharine, 73
Cornell University, 13, 99, 109, 149
Cotton Exchange, 65
Crawford, Joan, 47
Cronkite, Walter, 154
Crowell, Merrill, 75
Cuevas, Senora, 134-6
Cunard Building, 65
Curtis, Charles, 19
"Cutler Wholecloth," 153

Daily News, 68
Davis, David, 168
Dean, Abner, 79
Delta Upsilon, 86
Dickerman, Donald, 57
"Dunking Tank," 35
Durand, Ruth Sawyer, 154

Eakins, Thomas, 92
Emerson, Faye 163
Emmons, Frederick E., 170
Enchanted Schoolhouse, The, 154
Escher, John, 139
Esquire, 99
Everett, Julian G., 171

Fadiman, Clifton, 154
Farrand, Daisy, 53
Farrand, Livingston, 49
Fishback, Margaret, 82
Five Golden Wrens, 123
Flypaper Reports, The, 120-22

Ford, Corey, 72
Forrestal, James V., 73
Fosdick, Raymond B., 76
"Fountain of Youth" mural, 84-5
Francis, Arlene, 170
Frincke, Harold C., 175
Fuertes, Louis A., 22

Gallagher, Barrett, 101
Garrison, N.Y., 138
Garroway, David, 154, 163
Gatling, John, 171
"Ghost Painters, The," 149-153
Gish, Dorothy, 73
Gish, Lillian, 73
Globe and Square Dealer, The, 49-53
Goldwin Smith Hall, 45
Grand Central Station, 58
Greenwich Village, 65
Greta Garbo, 66
Guam, 133
Gurney, Paul, 40-42, 171, 175

Hallahan, Captain, 78
Hammond, William A., 53
Hanscom's Bake Shop, 80
Heigh-Ho Club, 57, 176
Henderson, Lyle R. C., 163
Hershey, Donald C. 36, 171, 175
Herzbrun, Philip, 157
Holland Tunnel, 106
Holmes, Ransom S., Jr., 52
Holsman, John T., 48
Holsman, William T., 48;
Hoy, David, 49
Hunt, Howard, 145

Ithaca High School, 176
Ithaca Journal, 91
Ithaca Yacht Club, 105, 176
Ivy Room, Willard Straight Hall, 140

Kellerman, Karl, 71, 172
Klug, Harry, 94

Lake Cayuga, 13
"Laughing Jack," 78-9
Lehigh Valley Railroad, 92
LeMay, Curtis, 126, 131-3
Lent, Robert J.F., 61, 65, 159
Lincoln Hall, 38
Lincoln, Paul M., 46
Lindbergh, Ann, 138
Lockwood, Henry S., Jr., 52
London Times, 150
Lott, Ruth Tompkins, 172
Luce, Clare Boothe, 87
Luce, Henry, 87

Manny Wolfe's Chop House, 72
Mark Twain, 91
Mark Twain Hotel, 91
Martin, Clarence A., 16, 161
Marx, Groucho, 97
Matteson, Howard W., 44
Maud for A Day, 104
Mayers, Robert A., 161, 172
McGraham, Agnes, 31
McGraw Hall, 13
Meredith, Burgess, 97
Metropolitan Life Ins. Co., 105
Miller, Norman A., 52
Milne, A.A., 124
Minelli, Vincente, 99
Minetta Lane, 67
Mitchell, Valerie Nield, 133, 172
Morgan, Henry, 154
Morrill Hall, 13
Moxley, Virginia Gray, 172
Museum of Modern Art, 55, 88, 104

New Year's card, 54
New Yorker, The, 99, 101
New York Herald Tribune, 105, 123
Nield, Walter K., 133, 165, 173, 175

Odell, Arthur G., Jr., 87
Owings, Nathaniel A., 55, 101
Oxford University Press, 113

Pearl Harbor, 117
Pentagon, The, 120
Pilots' Club, 78-9
Pius, Pope, 165
Poe, Edgar Allan, 100
Potter, Stephen, 154-7
Powell, John N., 73

Radio City Music Hall, 84, 100
Ranum, Arthur, 20
Rayburn, Gene, 139
Rayburn, Helen, 139
Reader's Digest, 136
Redden, Herman, 173
Rockefeller Center ,75
Rockefeller, John D., Jr., 75, 84
Roger Smith Hotels, 96, 176
Roller-skating in Grand Central, 45

Saipan, 126, 133
"Saloon de Garboon," 39
Sanford, Hilda Berry, 173
Saturday Evening Post, 145
Savoy Plaza Hotel, 86, 176
Scott, G. Norman, 59
Seagrave, Louis, 82
Seavey, David, 111
Seuss, Dr., 79, 86
Seymour, Alexander, 24
"Seven Secrets," 143
Sheridan Square, 66, 97
Sheridan Theater, 66
Short, Frederick W., 35
Sibley Hall, 38
Sidewalk Superintendents' Club, 76
Siebenthaler, George, 32, 175
Smith, Alfred E., 172
Spring Day Carnival, 46
Statues, Cornell, White, 36
Straight, Willard, 45
Subway Sun, 68
Sullivan, Frank, 72
Syme, Helen English, 40, 110
Syme, John P., 110

Syracuse American, 49, 51

Taylor, F. Chase, 83
Temple, Shirley, 124
Times Square, 101
Today Show, The, 154, 163
Toffenetti, Dario, 101
Toffenetti Restaurant, 101, 176
Tone, Franchot, 97
Town and Country, 145
Troy, Elinor, 30, 43
Troy, Elizabeth G., 175
Troy, Francis B., 30, 69, 117, 159, 174
Troy, Hugh
—as artist, 45, 57, 68, 79, 81-86, 96, 100-102, 138, 176
—as author, 104, 110, 123, 183-5
—birth, 176
—children, rapport with, 124, 133, 172
—Cornell years, 13-54
—death, 168
—family background, 176
—Garrison years, 138-143
—homes: Ithaca, 27; New York, 55, 61, 65, 67, 72; Garrison, 138 Washington, 145, 149, 165
—as hoaxer, prankster: Acheson, Dean, fishing, 161; "baby brother," 41; "barrell ascension," 38; beetle inspection, 106; bookmaker, plays, 65; bombing report, 131; bon voyage to Harry Klug, 94; boy through space, transfers, 47; breakfast at Seymour's, 24; Christmas card, fake, 83; CIA regulation, 147; "class picture," 32; clubwomen, lectures, 113; coins, hiding, 79, 80; "ceiling, fallen," 18; Cuevas, Senora, 136; demolition expert, 117; ducks in organ, 109; Fifth Avenue, digs up, 60; fish, takes orders for, 73; Flypaper Reports, conceives, 120; folklorist, dupes, 126; "getting grandmother behind," 30; Ghost Painters, 149; "girl" from convent, 30; *Globe and Square Dealer*, 49;

gold piece, see coins; goldfish, "eats," 77; hand, false, 108; hydrant, fake, 108; leg, false, 172; legless man, 14; mannikin in reception line, 172; mailbox, paints, 103; "measles," 170; moths in a movie, releases, 66; nude in the bath, 56; painting equipment, stores, 140; park bench "steals," 61; pearls in oysters, 77; pearls, broken string of, 170; Potter, parties for, 154; rhinoceros in lake, 22; rubbers, paints, 21; shoelace, ties, 174; statue footprints, 36; Today Show, April Fool on, 163; trolley shelter "privy," 45; Van Gogh's "ear," 89; West Point, wakes up, 141.
— humor, sense of, 31, 69, 79, 96
—marriage, 117
—military service, 117-136
—New York years, 55-115
—personality and character: 27, 31, 43, 45, 69-72, 97, 109; generosity: 68-9, 71, 96, 99, 159
—physical appearance, 16
—as raconteur, 59, 71, 77, 91
—Washington years, 145-168
Troy, Hugh, Sr., 25, 53, 93, 99, 153, 176
Troy, John P., 32
Troy, Mary Wall, 27, 91, 99, 176
Troy, Patricia Carey, 105, 117, 124, 138-9, 141, 154, 165-6
Troy, Rose, 93
"Troy's Thirty Acres," 72
Twain, Mark, 91

Undercover, 145

Vallee, Rudy, 57, 72
Van Gogh, Vincent, 88
"Van Gogh's Ear," 89
Wade, Harry, 41, 109, 174
Waldorf, Astoria, 98
Walker, James J., 67
Washburn, Kenneth L., 43
Washington Daily News, 151
Washington Post, The, 147-153
Washington Square, 67
Webb, Vanderbilt, Mrs., 138
Weekly Reader, The, 139
West Point, 141
White, Andrew D., 36
White Hall, 13-17, 32
Widow, Cornell, The, 46, 176
Willard Straight Hall, 45, 140
Wilson, Woodrow, 82
Winchell, Walter, 93
Winter, Ezra, 45, 55, 57, 65, 68, 83-4
Wolfe, Tom, 2, 7, 89, 122
Woodin, Royal H., 149, 167
Woodward, Alice, 75
World's Fair, 1939, 100
Wright, M. Birney, Jr., 52

Year of the Christmas Dragon, 154
Young America, 139

Zeissig, Alexander, 99, 105, 153
Zeissig, Edith Cuervo, 27, 99, 174
Zimmer, Emile J., Jr., 52, 174

The author presents his talk to a group in Baltimore, Maryland

About the Author

Con Troy was born and spent his boyhood in Elmira, N.Y. After attending Cornell with his cousin Hugh he was in charge of industrial sales for Pennsylvania Electric Co. Towanda, Pa., until 1954. He then served in Reading, Pa. as Industrial Sales Planner and Coordinator of Sales Training for Pennsylvania Electric Co. and Metropolitan Edison Co. and later as a project manager for Reading Industries, Inc.

Mr. Troy is an author of papers and magazine articles on lighting, vision, electric heating and abstract art. His hobbies include tape recording, and the building of silk screen equipment for reproducing his paintings and kinetic art which he has exhibited. He is a member of the Reading Chapter, Pennsylvania Society of Professional Engineers, a director of several organizations, a past director of the Pennsylvania Council for the Blind, and a past chairman, Eastern Pennsylvania Section, Illuminating Engineering Society.

Betty Troy is a columnist who has for many years written for the *Reading* (Pa.) *Eagle* and other papers. The Troys have two sons and live in Wyomissing, a suburb of Reading.

In 1976 Con Troy began six years of research for this book, visiting places where his cousin Hugh lived and worked, taking photographs, and interviewing over three hundred persons. A hundred of his pictures form a "Hugh Troy Exhibit" he often displays. He also uses eighty slides to present his talk, "Laugh With Hugh Troy, World's Greatest Practical Joker."

He publishes some of Hugh Troy's writings and a cassette in which Hugh Troy himself tells tales of many of his escapades. He may also publish certain of Hugh Troy's works of art and republish his children's books.

Con is still adding to his collection of Hugh Troy lore and invites readers who may have useful information to get in touch with him.

Cornellians Hunt Bradley '26 and Prof. Kermit L. Parsons '50 view a panel of the Hugh Troy exhibit presented by the author, right, in Barton Hall, Cornell University.

Colophon

Dear Reader:

*I designed and published this book for
    your reading pleasure. These people
    helped:*

*Prof. David Bullock, Kutztown, Pa.,
    created the title page and jacket.*

*Brophy's Composition Service, Sinking Spring, Pa.
    set the text in 11/13 Souvenir.*

*Forrest Miller, photographer, Reading, Pa.,
    prepared the illustrations.*

*Fairfield Graphics, the Arcata Group, Fairfield, Pa.,
    printed and bound it.*

*Did you enjoy reading it? If so, I'd like
    to hear from you.*

TROJAN BOOKS
1330 Cleveland Ave.,
Wyomissing, Pa. 19610

If you cannot buy this book elsewhere, you may
buy it from us. Write us for an order form.